Sociology
Looks
at Religion

Sociology
Looks
at Religion

J. Milton Yinger

THE MACMILLAN COMPANY, NEW YORK
COLLIER-MACMILLAN LIMITED, LONDON

Second Printing 1966

The Macmillan Company, New York
Collier-Macmillan Canada Ltd., Toronto, Ontario
Library of Congress catalog card number: 63-15705
Printed in the United States of America

Grateful acknowledgment is hereby made for permission to
quote from the following published works:

To Charles Scribner's Sons for permission to quote from
Reflections on the End of an Era by Reinhold Niebuhr; to
Journal of Social Issues for permission to quote from papers by
Robin Williams and James Coleman in Volume XII, no. 3, and
to the authors for their personal permission; to Holt, Rinehart,
and Winston, Inc. for permission to quote from *Escape from
Freedom* by Eric Fromm; to Doubleday and Company, Inc. for
permission to quote from *Protestant-Catholic-Jew* by Will Herberg, © 1955 by Will Herberg; to Yale University Press for permission to quote from *Millhands and Preachers* by Liston Pope;
to Beacon Press for permission to quote from *The Black Muslims
in America* by C. Eric Lincoln, © 1961 by C. Eric Lincoln;
to the Board of Directors of the Religious Research Association
for permission to reprint the 1962 Harlan Paul Douglass Lectures
which first appeared in the Winter 1963 and Spring 1963 issues
of the *Review of Religious Research*, copyright 1963 by Religious
Research Association, Inc.; to The University of Chicago Press,
publishers of the *Journal of Religion* for permission to reprint
"The Present Status of Sociology of Religion," by J. Milton Yinger,
Journal of Religion, Volume 31, No. 3, 1951; to *Daedalus* for
permission to reprint "Social Forces Involved in Group Identification and Withdrawal," by J. Milton Yinger, Spring, 1961, copyright by *Daedalus*; to *American Anthropologist* for permission to
reprint "The Influence of Anthropology on Sociological Theories
of Religion," by J. Milton Yinger, June, 1958, Volume 60, no. 3;
to *Sociology and Social Research* for permission to reprint "Areas
of Research in the Sociology of Religion," by J. Milton Yinger,
July-August, 1958.

Contents

Preface

THE PLACE of the study of religion in the social sciences has been a rather curious one. There have been ideological attack and ideological support, both under the name of a science of religion. There have been grand and often brilliant theoretical formulations. There has been a-theoretical description; and there has been vast neglect. But the "bread-and-butter" of any science—the testing of theoretically significant propositions by the use of controlled observation—has been in short supply.

Happily, this situation has begun to change. In Europe and America, the scientific study of religion has gained increasingly strong support since the Second World War. Easy generalizations about religious institutions and behavior are being replaced by careful comparisons. The need to take account of variations in class, education, and other social facts before generalizing about the influence of religion or influences on religion is increasingly recognized. Several specialized journals for the publication of the results of religious research have been established.

The kinds of questions raised by contemporary research in the sociology of religion indicate that it is not an esoteric specialty, working at the fringes of scientific interest. To study the sociology of religion is to work with

7

most of the major areas of current interest in the analysis of society and culture. Without careful attention to religious groups and behavior, one leaves serious gaps and weaknesses in his study of social stratification, social change, intergroup relations, political sociology, bureaucracy, community studies, social consensus and dissensus, the sociology of conflict, and the developmental processes in newly formed nations—to mention several areas of current research interest. The essays here presented may indicate the ways in which the study of religion is involved in several of these branches of contemporary sociology.

The chapters that follow are revisions of papers and lectures which I have prepared for widely differing occasions, but which, despite their diversity, focus on one central theme: the student of society must be a student of religion; and the student of religion must be a student of society. Chapter One was first presented as a Marshall-Wythe lecture at the College of William and Mary and appeared as a chapter in *Unsolved Issues in American Society* (R. Wayne Kernodle, editor; The College of William and Mary, 1960). Chapters Two and Three were presented as the 1962 H. Paul Douglass lectures to the Religious Research Association and were printed in slightly different form in the *Review of Religious Research* (vol. 5, nos. 2 and 3, 1963). Chapter Four was first prepared for a conference on Group Life in America sponsored by the American Jewish Committee. An earlier version appeared in *Daedalus* (Spring 1961). Chapter Five is a revision of a paper presented to the American Anthropological Association and published in *American Anthropologist* (vol. 60, no. 3, June, 1958). Chapter Six draws substantially on two papers, "Present Status of the Sociology of Religion" (*Journal of Religion,* vol. XXXI, no. 3, July, 1951) and "Areas for Research in the Sociology of Religion" (*Sociology and Social Research,* vol. 42, no. 6, July-August, 1958). Chapter seven was first prepared for the Division of Studies, Commission on Institutionalism of the World

Council of Churches. Although most of the papers have been extensively revised from their original form they are clearly based on the materials I have cited. I would like to thank the sponsoring groups and the journals where they have appeared not only for the right to use these articles but also for the stimulation and lively interchange that accompanied their original presentation. I hope that in revising them I have taken advantage of the discussion and communication that followed their first appearance as well as profited by new material that has since appeared. Perhaps in some small way these essays in this combined form can contribute to the vitally important analysis of religion in society.

J. Milton Yinger
Oberlin, Ohio

December 26, 1962

Foreword

FOR MOST people, religion is a faith to be lived—or perhaps to be neglected—but for a few, it is also a phenomenon to be studied, historically, philosophically, psychologically, or sociologically. When anthropology and sociology developed in the nineteenth century, religion naturally came into their view as one of the most significant aspects of society and culture. Even a quick glance reveals the universality of religion, yet the wide variety in the forms of its expression. So long as societies were in relatively infrequent contact with one another, these facts had little significance; but when contact became extensive, and when mobility and change created situations of religious diversity *within* societies, the facts of universality and variety became important. Some response to them was necessary. Perhaps the most common kinds of response to situations of interreligious contact are these:

The religions of others are wrong. I must oppose them or try to convert them to my way.

Religions, although different, are all to be understood as efforts to struggle with perplexing human problems—they are equally good.

Since the various claims to absolute validity are mutually exclusive and self-contradictory, religions are shown to be in error—they are equally false.

Religions share many things in common; they change and grow. But in terms of their values and their effects, they can nevertheless be differentiated. Sympathetic and informed value choices among religions are still needed.

The sociologist acting in his professional role takes none of these positions, although he may agree with one or another personally. (I would incline toward the last.) He too is impressed with the universality and the diversity of religion and is led to ask his particular kinds of questions. What functions does religion serve for society and for individuals—that is, to what degree does it keep them operating effectively? What are its possible dysfunctions? How can one account for the wide variety of religious belief and practice between societies and within societies? How is religion related to the secular beliefs and groups around it—to economics, politics, the class system, and the family, for example?

The scientific study of religion necessarily makes certain assumptions about religion. It does not claim that these assumptions are ultimately true, but simply asks: Can one, starting from these premises, say anything interesting and valuable about the subject under study? There is no pretense that this is the only way in which the data can be studied, no claim that all that can be said about a subject can be said by science. There is simply the affirmation that the methods of objective science can be applied to religious phenomena. This means that religion, when it is being examined within the framework of science, is dealt with as part of the natural world, subject to the laws of cause and effect and the rules of logic. There is no reason to be a halfhearted scientist here, looking upon the analysis of religion as somehow different in kind from other scientific work. One needs, to be sure, to be a modest scientist, for the subject is one of great complexity. What one can say confidently about religion on the basis of present knowledge is not a great deal, and what can be said about religion from nonscientific perspectives may well be more important. This is no reason, however, for the scientist to slip over into evaluative frames of reference. His procedures are inappropriate to the resolution of questions that arise from other perspectives. We can only try to say, as fully and accurately as possible: these things are true under this particular set of conditions. In the pages that follow there will be many propositions of this type, most of them to be taken as tentative efforts to state how religion and society interact under certain conditions. What we may *wish* would happen, whether a given development is a happy or an unhappy fact, how a specific piece of knowledge will be used—such questions cannot be resolved by science. It is doubtless true, however, that our religious responses to life will be more meaningful if they are based, not on ignorance, but on an understanding of the relationships of religion and society. The sociology of religion can be a valuable complement, not only to other sciences of religion, but to the religious quest itself.

I

The Sociological Interpretations
of Religious Movements

EVEN A quick glance at the headlines or a rapid tour through a growing city brings to prominent attention the place of religion in society. The Supreme Court interprets the First Amendment; Black Muslims produce a vivid radio drama; Negro and white "sit-ins" seek to break the segregation pattern; an evangelist holds a rally in Madison Square Garden; a modernistic church is built in a new suburb—and proves to be too small within five years. By such items, the intricate ways in which religion is involved in the life of a society are revealed. By exploring religious movements in their social settings we can begin to understand why they develop when and where they do. In the chapters of Part I, we will explore some of the religious consequences of the growth of cities, of minority status, of the decline of ethnic groups, of prosperity, and—most particularly—of rapid social change. These chapters are not research reports but interpretive essays, informed by the basic sociological premise that no social process can be understood if its social setting is disregarded.

1

Religion in Urban Society

IF A writer on art spent all his time analyzing the personality of artists, describing their relationships to various patron groups, and interpreting the connection between art and economic and political affairs, his readers might wonder what had happened to the core of his subjects—to art, pure and simple. Those most interested in art, most concerned to maintain and extend their conceptions of artistic excellence, might feel particularly uncomfortable with an external view that did not evaluate and did not try to evoke some of the emotional quality of artistic experience.

The same kind of objection can well be raised to any effort to study religion "at a distance." Does not such an approach miss almost all the important things there are to be said about religion? Can one see a stained-glass window from the outside?

I shall have to leave this question for you to answer. For what, indeed, I am going to try to do is to look at religion from the perspective of sociology, anthropology, and social psychology, to see it as one of the processes of social life. One need scarcely point out that this is a partial view, a modest approach. It can add significantly to our full understanding of the meaning of religion only

17

if its limitations are recognized. Yet I believe that failure
to use the resources of contemporary social science would
be to impoverish our understanding of religion.

I. The Sociological Approach
to the Study of Religion

The basic proposition from which a sociologist starts,
in his analysis of religion, is a simple one: Religion cannot be understood in isolation from the rest of society.
Religion is part of a system, affected by and affecting the
economic and political processes of society, the family
patterns, the technology, the nature of communities. If
one part of the system changes, all the other parts are
influenced in various ways. If men move from agricultural
villages to metropolitan areas, their religious life is vitally
affected. If literacy, mobility, science develop in a society,
its religions will undergo important changes, not simply
in superficial forms, but in fundamental ways. If a new
religion is vigorously introduced into a society, the whole
social structure will feel the impact, while at the same
time the structure will modify the religion it absorbs.

Closely related to this proposition is the concept of
functionalism. The basic parts of a social structure are
best understood as efforts to perform certain functions
vital to the life of society. According to this view, societies
are not as infinitely flexible as it once was thought they
were. Revolutionary movements, for example, may attack
the institutional structure of society—the state, the family,
the church. Owing to widespread alienation and strain,
the movement may succeed in winning power. The leaders
are likely soon to discover, however, that many of the
functions necessary to the life of a society can be performed only by reestablishing the institutions they ab-
horred—or some equivalents.

This concept applied to religion means that every

society will have a religion—even if it is called antireligion. It will, in other words, have some pattern of belief and action by means of which it seeks to perform certain vital functions. The religion may not be a very good one, in your judgment or mine; it may perform its functions poorly. But a society without some integrating system of values is a contradiction in terms.

This leads us, of course, to the problem of definition. Although it is tempting to take the referent of the word "religion" as self-evident, I fear that failure to make some effort to define our terms will weaken our ability to understand many developments in urban settings. Paul Tillich defines religion as "that which concerns man ultimately." This is very helpful, yet if we study religion comparatively we discover that there are important disagreements concerning the ultimate questions of life. At the heart of many religions, the ultimate question is: how will man spend eternal life. This is a central if not the central question of classic Christianity. One would hesitate to say, however, that most urban people think in these terms today. With respect to themselves they are more likely to ask of their religion that it help them grapple with meaningless suffering, with loneliness, with the sense that life is rudderless. To others, the ultimate questions have a group dimension: life in a society that crushes some of its members, deprives them of opportunity for full use of their capacities, causes one man to treat another ignobly, sets group against group—life in such a society threatens the ultimate values.

We can put this problem of definition in other terms. Most of us would agree that religion can be defined as a group-supported road to salvation. But salvation from what? There is wide disagreement, with beliefs varying with occupation, class, race, education, residence, and many other factors. We will be in a poor position to understand religion in urban settings if we believe that the ultimate problems from which man seeks salvation by religion are self-evident and universally shared, and that questions that we do not happen to regard as ultimately important are, by definition, not religion.

This point of view leads inevitably to the observation that religion is only one of many roads to salvation that man follows. He seeks salvation from ugliness, boredom, meaninglessness, and suffering in many ways that often blend into religion but are not identical with it. Religion may share with medical institutions the function of reducing ill-health and suffering in a society where little is known about the causes of disease; but religion will gradually relinquish this function to secular groups in a society where medical knowledge has grown large. In a situation where social change is far-reaching, religion will share with other movements a concern for some of the fundamental questions of meaning. We will be wise to realize this as we analyze religion in urban societies. It will be well to recognize how religion shades off into nonreligion and how it interacts with other efforts to grapple with our ultimate problems.

Paul Tillich makes this point well when he comments on the wide variety of beliefs and patterns of action that have sprung from the soil of technical society. Many of these are religious in only a remote sense, but they represent something of the same effort to resist the depersonalization, the loss of identity that we all are threatened with in modern society: Kierkegaard's religious existentialism was an effort to resist a world in which, as he saw it, everybody was being transformed into a thing. But his religious response to this situation was matched by a long series of secular efforts to resist the depersonalization. Marx by attacking the institutions he thought responsible for crushing the individual, Nietzsche by demanding self-affirmation in face of the dehumanizing forces of modern society, Freud by searching for a self that is uncoerced and spontaneous, Sartre by "isolating the individual from the embracing structure of technical civilization," these, and many other secular thinkers must also be studied in terms of their efforts to struggle with the meaning of life in modern society.[1]

II. *The City as a Setting for Religion*

If this point of view, sketched so briefly here, has any merit it will help us to understand some of the religious movements of our time. The major religions of the world developed, in the first instance, in rural societies. It has been scarcely a century since the first heavily urban societies began to develop; and even today, less than a quarter of the world's population lives in communities larger than 20,000 persons. Religion has been, and still is to a substantial degree, tied to rural societies. The growth of cities and the development of urban civilizations have posed enormous new problems for religious institutions (as they have for political, economic, and familial institutions). Many of man's ultimate problems remain the same of course: the disruptive fact of death, the bitterness that many feel when the ungodly prosper, the capacity we all have for aggression and a self-centeredness that weaken even our most cherished associations. But urban life also adds some new dimensions to age-old questions.

What aspects of life in urban societies are crucial for religion; what new experiences of man press in upon his received beliefs and demand their amendment if he is to feel at home in this new world? To put the matter in overly simple terms, urban society creates a situation where for the first time in human history individuals interact daily with strangers, with persons whose values and goals are significantly different from their own. Literacy and mobility expand the horizons of contact beyond anything the world has known, and with the contact have come disenchantment and secularization. This process is not new: Plato, looking with nostalgia at the coherence and solidarity of

Sparta, presumably in contrast to his beloved Athens, would create his ideal society in a spot where disrupting new ideas could not be borne in on "the bitter and corrupting sea." What is new is the scope of the influence of mobility and culture contact.

In the urban setting, kinship units lose some of their functions and their solidarity. We witness the rise of "mass" phenomena: media of communication reach millions of persons with the same message simultaneously; production techniques equip millions with nearly identical products. At the same time, paradoxically, we see the reduction of value consensus among those who are now more and more alike in superficial ways. In sociological terms, urban societies are characterized by greatly increased anomie—normlessness, value confusion. In such societies, individuals are much more likely to feel lost in "the lonely crowd," and to seek "escape from freedom," if I may use two well known titles.

We must not exaggerate the "anomic" quality of city life nor misinterpret its significance. There is a danger that what is in fact a new kind of social order will be seen as disorder because it is compared with a rural model. Although agreement on norms and values may decline in the city, functional interdependence and mutual tolerance increase. Moreover, many associations have developed that give structure and coherence to urban life. And despite the loss of some functions and the decrease in solidarity, the family remains a vital part of life in urban societies. Some earlier studies of the city mistook the effects of urbanization (the process of developing from a rural to an urban society) for the characteristics of a mature urbanism.

Keeping these qualifications in mind, we must nevertheless recognize that the rapid growth of cities has significantly changed the setting for human interaction. If my basic proposition is correct—that religious movements are vitally affected by the nature of the society in which they are found—the profound changes in the nature of life in urban societies must certainly have enormous consequences for religion. Many questions arise in connection with the application of this principle to American society: How are the anxieties felt by individuals being dealt with by various religious movements; what are some of the important value conflicts faced by religion today; what is the significance for the integration of a society that its members may be divided into distinctive religious groups—each claiming, at least to some degree—absolute validity?

Let me start with a sweeping generalization: Most of the vigorous religious movements in American cities reflect the efforts of various groups to come to terms with urban life, to feel at home in a sea of strangers, to find some stability in a setting where so much is changing. There is good evidence that the pentecostal sects, the small storefront churches, the revivals draw their adherents in large proportion from rural migrants. In the city they are confronted with a variety of new and difficult problems: they are part of a work machine that imposes its schedule upon them, their family patterns are disrupted, familiar associations in a close-knit neighborhood are destroyed. Having entered the city at its most poorly organized level, the lower-class migrant lacks meaningful social contacts. The established city churches are ill equipped to help him adjust to this new situation, because most of them are accommodated to the middle and upper classes in their form of worship, type of sermon, and group organization. Into this setting come the sects to declare to the migrant: You are not alone, life is not as baffling as it seems, your lowly status can be improved, if not on earth, then in heaven.

The small sects, as contrasted with the churches, have stern membership standards. One is admitted only after having given evidence of a religious experience and shown one's willingness to abide by the group's standards. Thus they say to one another: Despite the judgments of a wicked world, by religious standards we are the elite. Here is re-

ligion stepping into a situation where many people are
threatened with loss of motivation, with meaninglessness,
with a sense of their own worthlessness. To more sophisticated people, the fundamentalist theology, the drab
aesthetic standards, and the puritanical moral code of these
sects are repugnant. Before they are judged, however, perhaps one should ask himself what other alternatives are
available to those near the bottom of the economic ladder,
living in a society which trains its members to value confusion as much as to value integration, that stresses the
importance of "looking out for number one." Poverty,
powerlessness, and value confusion are harsh facts with
which every effort at response must start. Is it better to
join the "beat generation," to give one's self over to
cynicism, to join the four million worshipers (as contrasted with the sixty or seventy million users) of alcohol?
Better, perhaps, to face one's problems realistically and
try to overcome them. Better, of course, to create a society where poverty, powerlessness, and value confusion
are not found. But meanwhile? Perhaps the sects, for all
their intellectual, moral, and aesthetic weaknesses, are
significant social movements.

Although on the surface, middle-class religious developments seem to share little in common with the fundamentalist sects, they can equally be interpreted by reference to the social situations of their adherents. It is well
known that the "return to religion" in American society
in the last twenty-five years has drawn its support from
almost every level, and not least from the urban and
suburban middle class. Religious leaders are not certain
whether to applaud or lament the situation, but there can
be no doubt that church membership has gone up from
about half of the population over twelve years of age in
1940 to nearly 65 percent today. For the last several years
new congregations have been formed at the rate of 10,000
per year. Members are giving more money to religious
enterprises, are reading more religious books and articles,

attending movies with religious—and other—themes, and otherwise paying attention to religion to a degree far beyond that of a generation ago.

It is not difficult to develop a plausible thesis that the revival of interest in religion is a manifestation of the conflicts and anxieties of contemporary life. But it is important to remember that different groups have different kinds of anxieties and different preparation, by experience and culture, for various proposed solutions. Many middle-class persons, for example, are quickly tuned to Norman Vincent Peale's advice to "forget failure and go ahead." They have been trained to an individualistic and a fairly optimistic view of the world, and experience has at least partly confirmed the correctness of this view. Dr. Peale tells them that their troubles are not deep and the solution ready at hand: "Go to church at least once a Sunday for the next three months," follow these "7 simple steps." We are bombarded by similar advice with respect to commercial products dozens of times a day. "It is not surprising that persons raised on claims that a change to the correct facial soap can revolutionize one's chances for marital happiness, or to implications that if you improve your vocabulary by twenty words a day you may become a big executive, should respond favorably to 'the power of positive thinking.' " [2]

III. What Is a Religious Question?

In the city, religion is confronted with a series of problems from which it is relatively free in more static environments. It is generally believed that religion is "good for a society," that it softens some of the harsher consequences of the pursuit of secular values, that it makes it easier for diverse groups to live with one another without sharp conflict, because it emphasizes their common humanity. Who would want to live, one is often asked, in a community without churches? A careful examination of the role of religion, however, does not lead one to an unambiguous conclusion that it has contributed a great deal to the quality of life in urban settings. Difficulties that arise from the fact of rapid culture change, the daily interaction and interdependence of persons of different class and race, the continually shifting claims—as contrasted with static societies—for more favorable economic and political positions—such vital facts in the urban environment confront religions based on doctrines of universality with enormous problems.

Once again I must remark that those who define religion solely in terms of individual salvation are likely to dismiss this as an irrelevant statement. Economic and political questions are no concern of religion, they will argue; the growth of slums at the heart of our metropolitan areas is doubtless an unhappy event, but this has no bearing on problems of man's salvation. For my part, I doubt that one can separate the functions of religion in this way. In the search for some ultimate meaning to existence, some system of beliefs that lends dignity to life and makes its suffering less poignant, few men are likely to be persuaded by a religion that disregards the conflicts and the institutions that make life harsh and meaningless for many.

If one defines religion in this broader way—and each person will have to make his own decision concerning the appropriate definition—it becomes important to ask how churches have responded to some of the problems faced by our cities. In recent months there has been a great deal of discussion of the fact that despite ambitious plans for urban renewal, despite slum clearance programs and housing projects, despite the fact that we are talking about the richest nation in the world in the richest period of its history, the central areas of most of our metropolitan districts are deteriorating. The consequences are well known: physical blight is followed by disease, by delinquency and crime, by heightened racial conflict, by political corruption and value confusion. In such a setting, the gang, far more than the church, seems to offer some hope of salvation from a crushing situation. The gang says—as the church may say to a rootless young couple in the suburbs—you belong, you have a place; follow this code of loyalty and these values and together we can find some meaning, get some sense of importance, assert our own worth. Or at a later age, when ganging is no longer so easy, perhaps narcotics or alcohol will be used in a desperate effort to find a sense of well-being or a "peace that passeth understanding" in the midst of a society that has crushed one's sense of his own worth. I am not being merely impious when I use a scriptural quotation to try to capture some of the meaning of these activities. They can be fully understood, in my judgment, only by seeing them as religious substitutes—as the fumbling efforts of crushed individuals to find a road to salvation. The trouble is, of course, that they are mighty poor religions. One would scarcely expect a group of underprivileged boys to invent a glorious religion; but invent they will, if the established churches pass them by.

And that, with a few notable exceptions, is what they do. Usually, when an area of a city begins to deteriorate, churches resist the newcomers (who are almost always of lower status, and often of different race or ethnic group). And when they can resist no longer, the churches leave. Just when the stabilizing efforts of the churches are most needed, they head for the suburbs. There, people in more comfortable circumstances try to find a road to salvation that permits them to turn their back on the difficulties of the city, to disregard the harsh lives of many of their fellows. But the world is too interdependent. The disease, the crime, the political corruption, the racial conflict do not remain bottled up in the deteriorated areas. As the major religions of the world have long since affirmed—but each of us so easily forgets—one man's salvation is tied to that of his brother. "So send not to ask for whom the bell tolls, it tolls for thee."

Protestant churches have been particularly likely to turn away from the problems of the city. Many Protestant individuals and many denominations have a strong rural heritage which makes them feel ill at ease in urban surroundings. With Ogden Nash, they declare:

> The Bronx?
> No thonx.

In commenting on this question, Truman Douglass has pointed out some striking facts: In Cleveland, between 1920 and 1950, five of the largest Protestant denominations declined by 13 percent. Fifty-three churches left the heart of Detroit in a fifteen-year period. Between 1930 and 1955, while the population of the country was increasing by 19 percent, and its own membership by 41 percent, the number of churches related to one of the largest Protestant denominations declined, in 16 major cities, by 20 percent.[3]

There are exceptions to this trend of course. The East Harlem Protestant Parish in New York, for example, is now a thriving group of four churches, with over a dozen full-time people on its staff. They are working in an area where ten years ago not a single church was being supported by a major Protestant denomination. Here was a subcity of a quarter of a million people that had been completely bypassed by respectable Protestantism. In such situations, men do not give up the effort to find some dignity and meaning in life. They invent new modes of adjustment, they struggle with what they have, they strike back at a world that has treated them shabbily with whatever weapons are at hand—if not a coherent religion, perhaps a gang.

It wrenches our habitual way of looking at things to think of a delinquent gang as a quasi-religious effort to find some significance in life. We can perhaps understand it that way if we look at the world through the eyes of a gang member. The community gives him little help in solving any of his problems. He is bombarded by the sights and sounds of a wealthy society; he is told that the talented and the energetic can improve their lot; he internalizes many of the standards of the society around him. But the odds are enormously against him. He knows no one who has made a success according to this world's standards; he gets little family support; he learns little self-discipline, because the rewards that might establish his first feeble efforts at foresight are not forthcoming. For such a boy, the culture of the gang is quickly accepted as his response to life. It creates a situation in which the promises of self-esteem can be fulfilled; the standards of the dominant society are completely repudiated and very nearly their opposite accepted as the good life. Albert Cohen, in his excellent analysis of *Delinquent Boys,* correctly notes that this redefinition of the criteria of success is similar to the functions of some of the doctrines of Holiness Sects. ". . . They reverse the respectable status system; it is the humble, the simple and the dispossessed who sit at the right hand of God, whereas worldly goods, power and knowledge are as nothing in His eyes." [4]

IV. *Religion and Social Integration*

Such *ad hoc* religious developments may be thoroughly divisive forces in a society. In functional analysis, emphasis is given both to the possible contribution of religion to society (helping to furnish a basic value consensus and the ultimate standards on the basis of which difficult problems may be negotiated) and its contribution to individuals, in lending dignity and significance to their lives, even in the face of crushing difficulties. Almost all students of current religious movements in America agree that the societal aspects are vastly outweighed by the individual aspects. The reasons for this are clear: Urban life brings into daily interaction persons of widely different interests, values, and religious perspectives. Even among the adherents of a common religious tradition, Protestantism for example, differences of circumstance and of value are so great that unambiguous stands by churches, in an effort to integrate society, are seldom taken. It is not enough today for religion to give vitality and continuing support to a shared system of values: it must somehow negotiate among groups who have different values— with respect let us say, to business ethics or desegregation —in an effort to maintain in them a sense of their common humanity. When one adds to this difficulty the fact that modern communities are made up of persons of different religions as well, one has a situation where the ancient function of religion to unify a society is made almost impossible.

How have urban societies responded to these difficulties? A man from Mars might remark that the obvious solution is to invent a new religion, one free from the parochial loyalties and the limited perspectives of the ones we have inherited. But this is a step that few will take explicitly. The religions we have been taught embody our ultimate hopes and defenses against our ultimate fears. We may, indeed we do, redefine them slowly, but the change is usually carried on in the name of nonchange. The fact is that man has only partially left behind the values appropriate to the tribal societies in which he has spent most of his existence. Tribal societies are held together by kinship, by cultural uniformity, by shared fate; but modern societies are held together by political and functional interdependence despite the lack of kinship identity and in the face of cultural differences. To live in this kind of society requires some new values and some new religious perspectives.

How has urban man responded? To begin with, he

invented—slowly and painfully—religious tolerance. But tolerance leads a precarious existence, even in contemporary America. How can one be tolerant of persistent error—that is, failure to accept one's own religion—at the point of ultimate concern? Major religious differences can persist in a functionally unified society only at the cost of sharp conflict on the one hand or by the reduction of the significance of these religions to their adherents on the other, or by some mixture of these processes. Insofar as it is reduction in the significance of traditional beliefs that occurs, men do not thereby give up the search for a unifying system of values. They develop a quasi religion to do the job. Most often in our time it is nationalism, sometimes pursued with an almost desperate sense of urgency for the conviction of unity. Familiar religious elements become associated with the nation. Sacred writings, saints, ceremonies, demands for fervent expressions of loyalty to the nation as the ultimate object of allegiance appear.

Will Herberg has persuasively argued that in the very face of renewed participation in the work of the churches, the operative religion of many, if not most persons in this country is Americanism, not the beliefs and rituals associated with the traditional churches. If there is a "return to religion," the return is to an organization that makes few creedal demands and rouses in us few of the fundamental values around which our lives are built. There is probably a sense in which it is true to say that we are never tolerant about our basic values, our first premises. We can be tolerant of other religions because religion doesn't matter. If a man joins Kiwanis rather than Rotary we are ready to forgive him. Our opposition is reserved for those who do not accept the nation as their ultimate object of allegiance. In Will Herberg's terms:

It is the American Way of Life that supplies American society with an "overarching sense of unity" amid conflict. It is the American Way of Life about which Americans are admittedly and unashamedly "intolerant." It is the American Way of Life that provides the framework in terms of which the crucial values of American existence are couched. By every realistic criterion the American Way of Life is the operative faith of the American people.[5]

Thus the transformation of national sentiment into a quasi religion is one of the results of the great heterogeneity of our society. But different persons draw very different lessons from this development. Conservative religious spokesmen, particularly, but not only, among Catholics are likely to say that a genuine religious unity can be reestablished only if all Americans will accept the one true church (with, perhaps, some denominational differences within it, but no basic disagreements separating the branches). Others will contend that Americanism is not such a bad religion, after all, and that it contains the fundamental insights of the Judaic-Christian tradition within it. Still others believe that a vital religion for our time requires something new—either a little bit new, as in neoorthodoxy, or dramatically new—new enough to recognize that even the world religions are bound by their own myth systems and their traditions to particular societies or groups of societies.

I should like to return to this question in a moment, by way of conclusion to this chapter, but before we leave the topic of religious tolerance it is necessary to note that religious conflict has by no means been eliminated. It would be a mistake to press too far the thesis that Americanism is the basic religion, that the traditional religious beliefs have lost their vitality, despite the vigor of churches in our time, and that, therefore, religious tolerance is universal in our urban centers. Many people continue to use religion as the final arbiter of life's values, and insofar as they do, they are likely to be intolerant when basic issues arise. As Robin Williams says:

Beliefs and value-orientations regarding the nature of man, the problems of evil, the final ends of life—all the primordial questions—are not subject to immediate, pragmatic demonstration, in any sense. Yet they stand between the believer—the committed participant—and the agony, chaos, meaninglessness of an incomprehensible world. And, more positively, they define avenues of meaning, security, and fulfillment in an ordered life, transcending the "bare surface of things." . . . So conceived, we see again how differences that are defined as religious can come to have a peculiar acuteness and poignancy.[6]

Some kind of religious conflict is very likely in a complex society containing a variety of religious traditions. Sharp differences concerning the place of religion in the public schools, questions of censorship, birth control practices, balance in appointment to public office, and many other issues divide American communities along religious lines. We tend to minimize these problems by counting them to be the inevitable fruits of religious freedom. But if religion serves to divide a community, what has become of its function as the final arbiter of its values?

V. *Conclusion*

We have sketched a few of the religious processes characteristic of our urban society. But so far we have largely overlooked the thought of those who work with religion in intellectual and systematic terms, the theologians. While many persons of lowly status embrace the good news brought by Billy Graham and many middle-class persons seek salvation from the confusion, the nagging sense of inadequacy, the loneliness of modern life by following Dr. Peale's "8 practical formulas," or through the ministration of *Reader's Digest* and *Life* and the late Cecil B. De Mille, some theologians are calling for a much sterner religion. Heirs of an intellectual tradition that includes Kafka and Nietzsche, as well as Kierkegaard, draws on Darwin and Freud, Dreiser and Faulkner, as well as Barth, they emphasize the depth of man's problems. It is scarcely surprising in a century that has experienced two world wars, an extremely serious worldwide depression, the unbelievable brutality of Stalin and Hitler, and totalitarian suppression in many lands, that man's capacity for evil should come to dominate the thinking of many theologians. Not only the easy optimism of Peale and Daniel Poling and Bruce Barton, but the liberal theology that preceded their work comes in for sharp criticism by the neoorthodox thinkers. Until the nineteen thirties most American theological thinking had been moving in the liberal direction for a century. At least for those many individuals who were prospering in the new land and being touched by the intellectual currents of science, many of the established religious beliefs were losing force. "Saved by God's election" was a less congenial idea than Emersonian self-reliance. As someone has written, in this new setting, "God Himself became republican." The liberal movement had many diverse elements within it, but they tended to converge on opposition to predestination, to literal interpretations of the Bible, and to overemphasis on otherworldliness. There was a stress on those aspects of Christianity concerned with brotherliness and the idea that the kingdom of heaven is within you.

It is scarcely surprising that such an approach to religion should seem to be superficial and inadequate to many persons in an era of repeated worldwide tragedies. To Reinhold Niebuhr, tragedy is the central fact of human experience; religion, indeed, is a "citadel of hope built on the edge of despair." And the hope rests with God, not with man. Yet it should be noted that neoorthodoxy, if we may use that term to describe the broad range of contemporary thinking that emphasizes the depth of the human problem, does not give itself over to fatalism or a thoroughgoing pessimism. Niebuhr writes:

In the main body of Christian orthodoxy the pessimism in regard to the political order was too thoroughgoing to allow for a strong insistence upon individual rights. It was recognized that whatever the moral and spiritual ideal might be, in a "world of sin" individuals would always be claimed by societies and nations for the attainment of their own ends, and would sacrifice both their liberty and their equality to the necessities of the communal order. But in the sight of God individuals were to be regarded as still free and equal. The basic assumptions of an individualistic morality were, in other words, transmuted from socio-moral principles to religio-moral ideals. Naturally this solution of the problem led the church into premature compromises with the injustices and inequalities of society, but it was in many ways superior to modern liberalism in its recognition of the actual realities of life.[7]

In a period of such repeated crises as we have known, renewed attention to the darker aspects of human experience is bound to come into religious thinking. In the words of William James: "To ascribe religious value to mere happy-go-lucky contentment with one's brief chance at natural good is but the very consecration of forgetfulness and superficiality. Our troubles lie indeed too deep for *that* cure." [8]

We must grant that the neoorthodox and classical theologians force upon us an acute awareness of the tragic aspects of human life. But it is interesting, from the present point of view, to try to relate their work to the whole series of forces that influence man in modern society. One wonders if we do not see here a parallel with the experience of ancient Greece. There many had struggled, at the time of Pericles, to a view of the world free of fear and self-renunciation, yet well aware of the tragedies to which men are heir. But in the period of wars that followed, in face of the collapse of the *polis*, men "lost their nerve," as Gilbert Murray has described it. Out of the chaos came a renewed vitality for the mystery cults and a series of philosophies of defeat. Perhaps the world is witnessing something of a repetition of that situation. I have no competence to judge theological works as intellectual or religious systems, but perhaps I may be permitted to inquire about some aspects of their relationship to society and to the religious movements of our time. Theologians usually think poorly of the "folk religion," of the majority. As artists often abhor the taste of the masses, so theologians lament the taste of laymen in religious matters. They are unhappy about its practical, self-help quality and disdain its shallow intellectual content. Theologians work under a principle somewhat akin to parsimony in science—they seek to reduce religion to a few fundamental propositions, free from the "distortions" of particular times and places. Like parsimonious scientific principles, however, theological propositions are highly abstract. They are often emotionally unsatisfying and devoid of meaning to "the man in the street," who wants a religion that helps him to struggle with some highly specific problems. Because the abstract propositions of the theologians are unsatisfying, the "people" invent their own religions and they flock to the popular interpreters, largely unaware of the work of the intellectual leaders. Perhaps I am not being too impudent when I suggest parallels between Elvis Presley and Billy Graham, Pat Boone and Norman Vincent Peale, Andre Kostelanetz and Fulton Sheen, and Arturo Toscanini and Paul Tillich.

It is not for me, of course, to judge among these various religious styles. But perhaps I may be allowed to offer a layman's opinion. In the prestigeful neoorthodox theologies of the day, there is too much orthodoxy and not enough neo. They reemphasize the "tribal" differences among religions at the very time when diversified societies and an interdependent world need universalism. When Peale develops no dogma, no creed, but calls out to people "whatever your church," theologians shudder. When President Eisenhower asked that we all have a faith, "and I don't care what it is," religious critics throughout the land lamented the lack of standards. But what Peale and Eisenhower represent in this context is a kind of laymen's ecumenicalism, a folk effort, if you will, to reach across the traditional religious barriers that divide a society to give it again some sense of unity. The least common denominator of religious belief may be pretty low in our society, but it will not be raised by disregarding the need for a unifying frame of reference. If religious leaders continue to insist that, however valuable the partial insights of other sects and religions may be, only their own tradition contains fundamental religious truths, we will find folk religion and religious substitutes performing the integrating function of religion—and perhaps doing it very poorly. All the major religions, certainly including Christianity, are tied to tribal experiences that are defended as the source of absolute truth. Only when they all have been demythologized, to use Wilhelm Pauck's term, will they regain full relevance for the modern world.

With the destruction of isolation and the growth of persistent international contact, we are likely to witness in the next several decades a significant growth of a world culture, deeply affected by technology, mobility, literacy. If I may put the matter in technical sociological terms, the system requirements of an industrialized, interdependent world will strongly influence our present patterns of politics, economics, the family, and religion. Societies will become more nearly alike in many ways. Among the many critical questions that face us during this period, perhaps none is more important than the religious question: Will mankind find its way to a religion relevant to one world? The universalism of our "world religions" is partial: each is ready to declare that all men are brothers; but man's full salvation depends upon his acceptance of the declarer's own temporally and culturally bound revelations and traditions. The failure of religions to demythologize—to restate their truths in terms relevant to the life of modern man—will lead to increased weight being placed upon functional substitutes for religion, on nationalism particularly. The substitutes are likely to be substantially distant from the core values of the world religions. Only by major rethinking can these religions reestablish themselves as the spiritual sources of man in urban societies.

FOOTNOTES

1. Tillich, Paul, in J. A. Hutchinson, ed. *Christian Faith and Social Action.* New York: Charles Scribner's Sons, 1953, pp. 138-153.
2. Yinger, J. Milton. *Religion, Society, and the Individual.* New York: The Macmillan Company, 1957, p. 99.
3. Douglass, Truman B. "The Job the Protestants Shirk." *Harper's Magazine,* Nov., 1958, pp. 45-49.
4. Cohen, Albert. *Delinquent Boys.* Glencoe: The Free Press, 1955, pp. 122-123.
5. Herberg, Will. *Protestant—Catholic—Jew.* Garden City: Doubleday & Company, Inc., 1955, p. 88.
6. Williams, Robin M., Jr. "Religion, Value Orientations, and Intergroup Conflict." *Journal of Social Issues,* Vol. XII, no. 3 (1956), p. 19.
7. Niebuhr, Reinhold. *Reflections on the End of an Era.* New York: Charles Scribner's Sons, 1934, pp. 108-109.
8. James, William. *The Varieties of Religious Experience.* New York: Longmans, Green, & Co., Inc., 1902, p. 128.

2

Religion and Social Change: Functions and Dysfunctions of Sects and Cults Among the Disprivileged

THE COMPLICATED task of studying the subtle and intricate ways in which religion is related to society is made somewhat easier if we direct our attention to times of rapid social change. Because the forces producing change almost invariably affect the parts of a social system at different rates, and to different degrees, the mutual adjustment of parts that is relatively characteristic of stable periods in the life of a society is disturbed. Change may begin with technology, with increase of population, with economic improvement or decline, with growth of contact with other societies, with the pronouncements of a prophet, or in other ways. If the force of change is strong, strain is felt throughout the system. The introduction of contract labor patterns by Europeans into the villages of Melanesia upsets their patterns of authority and their marriage arrangements. Population growth among American Indians today makes their land base less and less adequate, forcing economic changes and migration. Transfer of Negroes from plantation areas into the hearts of our largest cities exposes their individual habits and group patterns, including their religion, to enormous strain. Thus institutional arrangements that are taken for granted or thought of as independent are brought forcibly to attention, by rapid change, as parts of a system. If the precise nature of their interdependence is not exposed by simple observation, at least the quality of societies as *systems*, not collections of separate institutions, is revealed.

Although this perspective is now widely shared among students of religion, there are enough disagreements that it may be well to state the logical possibilities in the relationship of religion and social change, and then to indicate the perspective of this essay. The possibilities are these: 1) There is no connection between religion (including its changes) and social change; they relate to different spheres of man's life. 2) Social changes (economic developments, growth of knowledge, shifts in technology, and the like) cause religious change. 3) Religious institutions and values prevent change in the society. Among those who hold this view, there are sharply contrasting values, ranging from the belief that religion "conserves the best" to the accusation that it is "the opiate of the people." 4) Religion initiates change; it is the independent variable, "the clue to history." Here again there is a range of evaluation. Communism is believed by some to be a "religious midwife" even though they regret the changes it brings about. On the other side are those who, interpreting their own religion, think of it as the major dynamic force for good in the world. 5) Religion is part of a complex interacting system. On some particular issue and from the perspective of a given point in time, religious developments may best be understood as responses to fundamental changes in their social environment. The new religious forces then "feed back into" the system from which they came, influencing the course of its development. On another issue, viewed again from a given point in time, religious change may be the dynamic factor. The influences thus set in motion become, in turn, conditioning and constraining forces that affect the religion which released them.

It is from this fifth perspective that I shall examine some of the phenomena of change in an attempt to analyze and interpret them sociologically.

I. *The Secular Setting of Sects and Cults*

Among the most interesting of the religious developments in the modern world have been the sects and cults that have appeared among groups caught in conditions of severe disprivilege. Frequently these are racial or cultural minorities who have been overrun by a militarily and industrially more advanced society or a more powerful segment of their own society. Prerequisites to their traditional way of life are destroyed; belief in the efficacy of the old ways declines; values and desires are taken over from the powerful intruding force; and yet full acceptance of the new way—including its religion—is neither possible nor permitted.

Responses to these conditions of "cultural shock" range from personal demoralization, to traditional reaffirmation, to aggression against the invading culture, to acculturation and assimilation. Our primary interest is in religious movements that arise in such contexts. Because these religions are frequently bizarre from the perspective of both the traditional culture and the powerful invading one, they are likely to be dismissed as aberrations. Because they may involve a strong emphasis on group conflict, the new religious movements may be lamented and sharply curtailed by those in power. From the point of view of the sociology of religion, however, such interpretations and responses seem insufficiently aware of the possible functions of sects and cults in aiding individuals and groups to deal with the world around them. In particular, the nature of their influence can adequately be understood only if it is studied in the light of available alternatives: How would the individuals and groups in question respond to the dramatic changes in the world around them if the religious movement in question were not available?

To answer this question, it is well to remember that there are certain facts in the situation which are scarcely subject to change by the disprivileged group. Any individual or social development must be carried on in the context of these facts. Whether one is dealing with tribal societies among the Melanesian Islands, with American Indians, or with peasant Negroes suddenly transferred to an industrial, urban world, these things are true:

The old way of life has been brought under severe pressure and can no longer be maintained. Traditional religious beliefs and practices, embedded as they were in the old order, lose their appeal. A new style of life, including a new religion, is needed; yet the religion of the conqueror, though often strongly urged upon them by missionary activity, is not fully meaningful and adequate. It is embedded in the whole social system of the dominant group—a system only partly experienced and understood by the conquered or minority groups.

The traditional separation of individuals and tribes imposes serious problems in the new context. Formerly separate, and even antagonistic, groups now find themselves caught up in a common situation. Unifying themes are needed.

Personal demoralization, in the several meanings of that phrase, has become more common. Perhaps two aspects are most critical: a growing gap between what individuals hope for in life and what they expect weakens motivation; and, in the more literal meaning of the term "demoralization," the breakdown of the old order has left many individuals without a coherent value system.

Religious innovations are not inevitable under these conditions, but the strains the conditions impose add new dimensions to the age-old problems of salvation. Among the many ways of struggling with the new situation, religious movements occupy a prominent place.

It is the thesis of this chapter that religious cults and sects—even those that seem most bizarre and carry most seriously the threats of conflict—have at least the potentiality of helping to carry their members over into a new life. In situations that demand rapid change, including drastic reorganization of personality, religious movements can serve a bridging function. They contribute to the breaking of ties to a crumbling old order and to orienting to the new order in a way that helps individuals and groups to maintain a sense of control and of dignity. They may help to forge a new unity to replace group lines that are obstacles to life in the new setting.

This bald statement of functions requires qualification of course. Many of the functions are latent and can be discovered only by a study of consequences, not by a study of the manifest content of the religious movements. The functions are probabilities, not certainties, depending particularly upon the responses of the surrounding society. Whether the potentialities for conflict carried in the themes of the Black Muslims, for example, develop into a significant aspect of the group's behavior depends more upon the surrounding society than upon the group's doctrines. And further, by way of qualification, a "bridging" sect or cult will build its way of life out of materials at hand. If a magical view of the world is powerful among its constituents, for example, it will not create a religious system free of magical elements.

II.   *Illustrations of Religious Protest*

In the descriptions that follow, I shall disregard the extensive differences among several movements in order to highlight the interesting similarities. If I move rapidly from group to group, without full attention to important differences, it is because I am interested in developing a theory of religion and social change in this essay, and am less interested here in discussing the full range of a particular group's characteristics.

For over three-quarters of a century the islands of Melanesia have been swept by millenarian movements that demonstrate how sensitively religion registers the currents of change. Instability in the European-dominated economy has created hardship for many of the islanders and undermined their confidence in rational planning to satisfy their needs. A great demand for labor in the mines and plantations has drawn large numbers out of their tribal societies for years at a time. Harsh recruitment methods, dreary barracks life, low pay when set beside the new-found wants, forceful domination by the white man, and bitterness at the deterioration of their own cultures have created powerful antiwhite hostility. Contrasts between the values of the white plantation overseer and the teachings of the missionaries added confusion. In such a situation, the native could not go back—the white man had not only disrupted his societies, but also had given him new wants and new values—nor could he go ahead, for his pay was minimal, his opportunities few, and his command of the white man's ways entirely marginal. "The stage was truly set . . . for the development of independent native movements, and for the casting of social and economic aspirations in religious form. . . . The hysterical phenomena found in most of the cults . . . are the product of the ambivalent attitudes and feelings of men torn between hatred of the White people who had destroyed the old way of life and who now dominated them by force, and the desire to obtain for themselves the possessions of these very Whites." [1]

Early religious responses to such a situation tended to be nativistic and revivalistic.[2] The old order, it is affirmed, will be reestablished and the invader driven from the land. In 1877 and the years following in Fiji, for example, a self-proclaimed prophet declared that the order of things would soon be reversed, ancestors would return to the island, and independence would be restored. "Eternal life and eternal pleasure were to be the lot of the faithful. For the aged, youth would be renewed and desire would return. The shops would be jammed with calico, tinned salmon and other goods for the faithful, but unbelievers would die, or be condemned to everlasting hell-fire, or become the slaves and servants of believers." [8] The white men would be driven into the sea.

In the decades that followed, cults in many parts of Melanesia developed along similar lines. In many of them the theme of "stolen Cargo" became prominent. From the point of view of the natives, as Worsley tells us, the white man received his vast supply of goods by steamer or plane from unknown lands. They did not manufacture them, and they merely sent back scraps of paper. It was not difficult for the natives to believe that the goods were made by their own ancestors and stolen from them by the whites, who had control over some secret. The secret was obviously not work. Prophets appeared to reveal the way to secure the cargoes and to reestablish native supremacy. Many systems of belief and ritual were propounded as ways of doing what, to the prosaic eye, seemed impossible—the defeat of the white man and yet the mastery of his secret for obtaining the vast cargoes from ship and plane. The Cargo cults often have led to tension, if not to open conflict with white overlords; they encouraged persons to neglect their gardens and other economic activities. On the other side, however, these cults contributed to the breaking down of village and tribal barriers that prevented effective joint action to deal with their new and shared fate. During a difficult period of transition they helped to prevent serious social disorganization by supporting belief in the ancestors and reduced personal disorganization by maintaining hope.

Although there are significant differences, much of the description of the Cargo cults can be applied to the Ghost Dance among some American Indians. We find again a background of cultural confusion, white domination, economic instability, and inability to carry out the traditional ways. Many prophets appeared in this setting, calling for a revival and describing the beliefs, group patterns, and dances necessary for salvation. As Lesser describes it with reference to the Pawnee in 1890: "Into this situation of cultural decay and gradual darkness, the Ghost Dance doctrine shone like a bright light. Indian ways were not gone, never to be recovered. Indian ways were coming back. Those who had lived before in the 'golden age' were still carrying on old ceremonies, old dances, old performances, and old games in the beyond. They were coming back; they were bringing the old ways and the buffalo. Dance, dance, dance. The white man would be destroyed by a great wind." [4]

Such religious attacks on the dominant society are not limited to conquered peoples. If, within a society, a group lacks an independent and successful past which can serve as the focus of the millennial dream, they can affirm that they are the true defenders of a tradition shared with their oppressors, who have fallen into sinful ways; they alone are "Jehovah's Witnesses." Such proletarian movements, in the sense that Toynbee, Cohn, and others have used this term, are in a society, but not of it. They are scarcely less critical of the existing institutions than a conquered tribe. This world, they declare, is full of sin and it is doomed. From all the ages, 144,000 are destined to rule with Jesus; but others who accept the Witnesses will live forever and enjoy a heaven without sin and trouble.[5] "The poor are going to become rich, the downtrodden are to be raised above the mighty, the sick and frail are to be made whole, the aging and the old are to become young again!" [6] Thus the Jehovah's Witnesses also attack the rich and powerful, although there is no race theme involved, as did the members of the Fiji Tuka Cult and the Indian Ghost Dance; and they attack the society by downgrading its institutions and refusing to accord it final loyalty.

Continuing to overlook the important differences, let me describe still another interesting religious movement in such a way as to emphasize its similarities with those just commented on. The Black Muslims, like the Jehovah's Witnesses, are in but not of American society. Like the Indian and Melanesian cults, they emphasize a race theme. Like them all, they point to the past, but always in a way that shows their great concern for the present and the future. For past glories, one might have expected American Negroes to renew a sense of identity with African Negro societies, as the Ras Tafari Cult in Jamaica has done, for example. But this would keep alive the very Negro identity that the Black Muslim movement seeks to destroy. Hence the themes: We are the lost nation of Islam; our salvation rests on the rediscovery of this tradition. All science is the product of the discoveries of twenty-four original black scientists, thousands of years ago. By redefining one's racial identity, by repudiating the white man's religion and attacking him as a knave, the 100,000 or more members of this movement seek for salvation from their soul-crushing lives. Most of the members are recent migrants into large cities, where their old accommodative patterns of life have been destroyed, their aspirations raised, their sense of power enhanced. Yet the painful facts of disprivilege and discrimination remain. It is in this context that the young, mostly male, mostly lower-class, often functionally illiterate Negroes join the Black Muslims. In Eric Lincoln's words: "The true believer who becomes a Muslim casts off at last his old self and takes on a new identity. He changes his name, his religion, his homeland, his 'natural' language, his moral and cultural values, his very purpose in living. He is no longer a Negro, so long despised by the white man that he has come almost to despise himself. Now he is a Black

Man—divine, ruler of the universe, different only in degree from Allah Himself. He is no longer discontent and baffled, harried by social obloquy and a gnawing sense of personal inadequacy. Now he is a Muslim, bearing in himself the power of the Black Nation and its glorious destiny. His new life is not an easy one: it demands unquestioning faith, unrelenting self-mastery, unremitting hatred." [7]

III. Patterns of Change Among Religious Protest Movements

Such religious movements, or religiopolitical movements, in a minority or suppressed group are usually impermanent. Whatever they may do to maintain or restore self-respect and to achieve group solidarity (that is, however much they may be functional for the minority), they are seldom regarded with favor by the dominant groups. Insofar as they mount an attack on the society or deny the validity of its basic values and institutions, they are scarcely functional for that society. Even in societies where freedom of religion is the rule, there is little tolerance for those efforts to win salvation that involve direct attack on the social order, including the dominant religious organizations. Almost universally, the response of those in power is suppression, the jailing of leaders, the curtailment of activities. Through the years, many of the leaders of the Cargo cults in Melanesia have been jailed and the movements suppressed. The Ghost Dance was smashed militarily at the battle of Wounded Knee. Hundreds of Jehovah's Witnesses have been jailed in the United States because their search for salvation involves a sharp disagreement with dominant institutions. Although there has as yet been little suppression of the Black Muslim—their attack having been almost entirely verbal—they are kept under close scrutiny.

By the nature of their relationship to society, then, the "attack" type of sect or cult is fairly short-lived. In an analogy from physical chemistry, one might say that it is a "radioactive" group with a short half-life. It tends to break down into a more stable isotope. Yet it is true, if you will forgive me for pressing this figure of speech one stage further, that this spinning world is a kind of sociological cyclotron that continually creates new "radioactive" material. If a sharply protesting religious movement is suppressed while the basic forces which produced it remain in operation, the group will reappear, in ever new guises, decade after decade.

It is often true, however, that the conditions from which unstable attacking sects and cults developed do not remain the same. Because of the influence of the religion itself on the members and because of changes in the surrounding society, more stable religious forms tend to appear. Although empirically there is often a mixture of types of response, two basic varieties of religious groups tend to follow a vigorous protest movement: If hope for restoration of an earlier culture and independence fades, the way is paved for a more accommodative religious movement. It may be more otherworldly in goals, or more reformist (as contrasted with the revolutionary implications of the attacking movements), or both. If, on the other hand, there is a growth in hope, if there is status improvement— perhaps as a result, in part, of the influence of the religious group itself on its members—the transition is likely to be toward a religious orientation close to that of the dominant members of the society; that is, the familiar sect-to-church transition takes place. Further search for greater income and power is carried on by more distinctly economic and political means.

There is no clear pattern of evolutionary stages in this sequence of events. Dramatic social changes and culture contacts may continually create the context for the emergence of new protest movements, as the history of Christianity so vividly shows. An important question emerges from the study of this process: What are the conditions under which a relatively stable accommodation will emerge; when will assimilation (the sect-to-church transition) occur? A reference to specific movements may help us to explore this question.

Among American Indians, religious movements have occupied an important place in the search for adjustment to the new world created by the coming of the white man. Military and symbolic efforts to reestablish Indian supremacy were doomed to failure. In several different settings they have been followed by religious movements that emphasized personal salvation, social reform, and peaceful acceptance of the white man, not Indian restoration and hostility to the newcomer. These religious movements have helped to shape the new values and the new personalities needed for life in a society where the old Indian ways were clearly gone (for better or worse). They have served, to use the concept introduced above, a "bridging function." Military defeat came first of all to the Indians in the Northeast section of the United States, and in this area appeared the first prophets calling for peace, reform, intertribal harmony, and personal morality —often in terms of an interesting Christian-Indian blend. Voget describes the situation well: "What succeeds now [after failure of efforts to reestablish Indian supremacy] is a new social and psychological configuration in which the self-that-failed fills the stage of individual and group consciousness. The battleground of human failure and success shifts from a struggle against external forces to a struggle against the self. Assuredly external forces that threaten are always there and must be met, but they are not now met with a mobilization of physical armament. The prophets of reform who come to herald the new day are men of peace, like Handsome Lake, teacher of the Great Message to the Iroquois. At a time when the 'Shawnee Prophet' and Tecumseh were beating the drums for

European destruction and Indian restoration along Ohio war trails, Handsome Lake called for peace and personal moral reform." [8]

The religion of Handsome Lake sought to validate a new personality and a new social order. His fellow chieftains were reactionary (in the purely descriptive meaning of the term—they wanted to reestablish Indian supremacy); but in that direction lay only destruction. His Great Message movement emerged from the contemporary scene. It was supported—as religious movements must be among Indians, as in so many other societies—by revelation. As in so many situations, it took a religious movement to supplant a religious movement, or more accurately, a social system buttressed by religion.

Did the Great Message of Handsome Lake succeed? The answer depends, of course, on one's definition of success. If one means: did it allow the continuation of Indian societies in their drastically altered environment, thus rescuing them from total destruction, and did it give to individuals a new dignity and self-respect in the context of vast cultural confusion, suffering, and demoralization, the answer is yes. It served and serves these functions reasonably well. "Through the Great Message the Iroquois have been able to maintain a firm continuity with the social past and to invest it with contemporary meaning. What they lost in status associated with war, hunting, shamanism, and the like, they gained back through the Great Message. Self and social self remained united, but in a new context." [9] If one means by success the relatively graceful destruction of Indian societies and the absorption of individuals into the dominant society, the Great Message of Handsome Lake has failed. But such a test would be to stretch the meaning of functionalism severely and perhaps to distort it with an ethnocentric bias.

A century after these events among the Iroquois, a similar sequence of Indian movements developed among the Plains tribes. I have commented briefly on the Ghost Dance as a religiopolitical effort to recapture the land from the white settler and to reestablish Indian power. When it was defeated, there emerged among many of the same tribes the Peyote Cult, a peaceful, accommodative movement whose most obvious feature is the search for peace by consumption of the peyote button (a form of cactus) with its narcotic effects. This religious movement has also served a number of functions for tribes and individuals: the playing down of intertribal conflicts, union of Christian and Indian elements, elimination of organized hostility toward the white man—which in its earlier forms was leading only to destruction—and the recovery of a system of values. In Spindler's terms: "Identification with Peyote literally saves the self and gives it sanctions and directives for an integration of conflicting cultural patterns." [10]

To describe the functions of the Peyote Cult is not to say that it is good. A functional description means simply this: Granted the conditions facing the Indian tribes involved, Peyote permitted a viable adjustment of their cultures and a manageable situation for them as individuals, while allowing them to continue to be Indians. The alternatives are to fight (either militarily, or in such religious terms as the Ghost Dance), to give up in the face of culture shock, or to assimilate to the ways of the white man (if he would permit it). Functional analysis says only that a given response does, or does not, serve to keep a group in working order and its members adjusted to their life conditions as they exist. To determine whether Indians *should* have accepted the Peyote Cult requires some declaration concerning the desirability or undesirability of their continuing to live as Indians in the cultural sense.

These brief remarks concerning some of the American Indian religious movements may indicate the course of events when a group is subjected to defeat. This same story has vast implications for the interpretation of the "world religions," of course, but I shall resist the temptation to develop the parallels here.

Many religious protest movements take a different line of development from that of passive accommodation. In terms somewhat overly sharp, one can say: If the protesting group is a subordinate segment of a society rather than a conquered society (e.g., lower-class city dwellers in the United States rather than an Indian tribe), and if, partly because of this fact, they draw their religious protest from the same religious tradition accepted by the dominant group (in contrast to the syncretist movements so characteristic of African Negroes, Melanesian islanders, and American Indians, for example), then the protest movement will tend to move in the direction of assimilation rather than accommodation. Conflicts with the established order will be abated; the group may become a church.

This is not, of course, a foregone conclusion. Results as various as Methodism and Quakerism (which I will call a denomination or class church and an established sect, respectively) can occur. A central problem in the sociology of religion is the specification of the conditions under which the one or the other of these patterns of development will take place. As a merest hint, one might propose the hypothesis that the depth of the original alienation from society represented by the religious protest will strongly affect the course of its development. Quakerism, heir of the radical attacks on English society in the seventeenth century, represented severe alienation. Winstanley's call for political and economic revolution was transposed, although not entirely, into a call for religious "revolution." One is tempted to draw a parallel between the situation among the radical protest movements in England in the seventeenth century and the shifts that took place among the Iroquois mentioned above. In Voget's words:

"If the social system of the Iroquois during the eighteenth century can be described as political first and religious second, after Handsome Lake the relationship was reversed." [11] The parallel would read: If the attacks on the English social system before the Civil War were political (and military) first and religious second, after Fox, the relationship was reversed.

This is too neat a formula of course. Our types never represent the complexity of the empirical world adequately. It would be fair to say, however, that Methodism expressed a far less sharp critique of the secular world than Quakerism. ". . . The Methodist movement remained throughout its history in the control of men who had been born and bred in the middle class and who were impressed not so much by the social evils from which the poor suffered as by the vices to which they had succumbed." [12] As a general principle, those sects develop into churches which from the beginning emphasized problems of individual anxiety and guilt, with the implication that these lead to social ills. Those that emphasized social evils first, with the implication that they are the source of individual anxiety and sin, tend to develop into established sects.

Many groups are difficult to classify according to this principle. The Jehovah's Witnesses, for example, seem nearer to seventeenth-century Quakers than to eighteenth-century Methodists, but there are aspects of both. We should also qualify or refine this principle in two ways: it may often be that a religious organization will move from sect to church (from sharp conflict with major social institutions to acceptance of them), but that individual members will not. Bureaucratic processes of accommodation may take place on the organizational level which do not touch the lives of the individual members. They drop out, often to search for another movement which properly represents or helps them to struggle with their sense of alienation from society. On the other hand, an unintended consequence of the teachings, even of the most radically protesting sect, may be to establish values and personality tendencies that lead to success in society, and thus to the likelihood that its norms and institutions will be more fully accepted.[18]

IV. Religious and Secular Alternatives

The analysis of a sectarian religious movement is strengthened by seeing it, not only in the larger secular context but also in comparison with or contrast to other modes of response among the members of the group being studied. The contemporary Black Muslim movement, for example, is more adequately interpreted if we study it in connection with other religious and secular processes among American Negroes. Even a quick glance at the headlines tells us that Negroes respond to their disprivileged status in America today in vastly different ways, ranging from well-disciplined "freedom rides" to utter demoralization. It is difficult to impose a system of classification on the wide variety of activities, but let me attempt to do so by ranging them along two variables: hope and discipline. On the basis of these two variables, one could describe four possible types of religious activity or of functional alternatives to religious activity. There could be movements which expressed neither hope nor discipline, others that expressed hope but not discipline, discipline but not hope, and both hope and discipline.

One can place various contemporary protests among American Negroes in each of the four type positions created by these two variables. This is an obvious oversimplification, but if used with care the procedure may help to clarify the concept of functional alternatives. The following chart shows the logical possibilities and notes groups that approximate them.

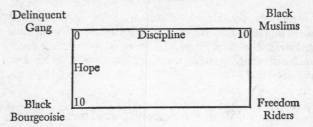

I would like to inquire whether, viewed in this context, two religious movements that seem to be extreme forms of protest do not take on a different appearance. It is possible that, granted the facts of American life today, they represent considerably more constructive developments than alternative roads to salvation.

Delinquent gangs are by no means a monoply of Negroes of course, nor even of the disprivileged, but they represent one of the efforts of some boys and young men to struggle with the sense of powerlessness, low status, and frustration. In *Millhands and Preachers*, Liston Pope described the way in which the small sects of the millworkers substituted religious status for social status—the last shall be first. In Chapter One I noted that a gang, with its own system of norms and values, can also be seen as an effort to find salvation from a crushing life. From one point of view the values and activities of the gang declare: "If we can't find some sense of dignity and cannot struggle with our most serious problems by means demanded by the dominant community, we will support or create a group whose standards we can meet." The standards of a gang may be not only different from, but also in many ways exactly the reversal of those of the "respectable" community —a drastic contraculture.[14] The full reversal of many values leaves a hint that the gang members do not have confidence in their own road to salvation. They have to repress the more standard values by denying them completely.

In a perceptive account of Negro responses to their status

in New Orleans, Rohrer and Edmonson describe the gang, one of their five types of "subcultures," in terms that clearly mark it as a religious substitute. The very grounds of self-respect are lacking for most lower-class Negro men. In the female-dominated families they have no way to learn what it is to be a man. The churches of the community are fatally identified in their minds with white domination and effeminacy. If salvation is not to be found in church, community, or family, it will have to be fashioned *ad hoc*, in terms of the conditions they face. "The psychic economy of the gang demands aggressive independence, a touchy and exaggerated virility, and a deep protective secrecy. Acceptance by the gang provides almost the only source of security for its members, but such acceptance is conditional upon continual proof that it is merited, and this proof can only be furnished through physical aggressiveness, a restless demonstration of sexual prowess, and a symbolic execution of those illegal deeds that a 'sissy' would not perform." [15]

Granted the conditions that exist—the crushing burden of prejudice and discrimination, the ignorance and poverty that follow in their wake, the unstable, female-dominated family (a heritage of slavery and the discriminations that followed it)—and one can readily see the gang as a "necessary institution," as Rohrer and Edmonson put it. Unhappy as are many of its consequences, by generally accepted standards, it may actually serve to curtail a more abysmal deterioration and alienation. That is about all that can be said for it, however. As a religious substitute it hardly ranks high. For that reason, we should be particularly interested in a slightly more orthodox religious movement that springs from the same vastly difficult conditions. The Black Muslims also draw most of their members from lower-class Negro males, some of them with criminal records, all of them struggling for a sense of dignity in an environment that gives them little help. They emphasize virility and toughness as the gang does. Without such an emphasis they could scarcely appeal to the same kinds of persons. If the hatred they express, the threats of violence, the demands for one-fifth of the country, and the extravagant interpretations of history seem both absurd and dangerous, we might be wise to ask what the alternatives are. Should we expect Negroes who have escaped the isolation of the plantation and discovered with their own eyes and ears the promises of a democratic and wealthy society to continue to accept unalloyed otherworldliness? Should we expect them to accept enthusiastically Christian churches which are fully implicated in segregation and discrimination? If it is granted that those choices seem unlikely, at least for many, perhaps we should ask whether we prefer the gang pattern, or alcoholism, or drug addiction, or utter demoralization. These may be the only real alternatives to the Black Muslims, or similar movements, for many persons.

What I am suggesting is that if you strengthen the gang —or the kinds of persons attracted to the gang—with dreams and discipline, but little hope, you get the Black Muslims. Arm them with hope as well, and you may get the freedom riders. But one finds few freedom riders among the functionally illiterate and deeply frustrated residents of our slums. For them, it is already a long religious step from the gang to the Black Muslims. In the group they are learning to plan, to sacrifice, to share and commune with others. These changes can serve as a bridge to fuller participation in the larger society, despite the explicit attack on that society. Through the Muslim symbolism, the selection of a new name, a new homeland, and a new group identity, deeply frustrated and self-hating persons see some hope of salvation.

We should be careful not to exaggerate the extent to which the Muslims break away from the dominant values and even the dominant religious themes to which many of them have been trained. Although the sect explicitly repudiates Christianity—"the white man's religion"—its appeal draws much from the Christian doctrine of rebirth. The ideology is not "otherworldly" in the usual sense, but for all of its castigation of Christianity—and of Negroes who accept it—the symbolism of the Black Muslims is not so far from that expressed by "my home is over Jordan" as it appears at first glance.

From the perspective of the sociology of religion, the Black Muslim movement is the kind of religious protest one would expect in an uprooted, disprivileged group, made suddenly aware both of the American dream and of the forces preventing them from sharing it. Add to this the exciting rise to independence of the African states and the relative indifference of Christian churches to discrimination, and the development of such a vigorous religious protest is readily understood. Its long-run consequences depend, to an important degree, not on its intrinsic qualities and internal forces, but on the larger American environment. It seems to be bringing a measure of solidarity to persons formerly divided and isolated in a hostile world. The stress on "black supremacy" is better understood as a radical religious attack on the inferiority complex of American Negroes than as an attack on the white man. Muslim doctrines give religious sanction to norms of behavior required by the larger society. Because these sanctions arise from a new religion, they do not seem to represent capitulation to the standards of discriminatory whites. Thus stable family patterns, thrift, responsibility on the job, and temperance are demanded as *Muslim* virtues. "Specifically, Muhammad denounces the matriarchal character of Negro society; the relative lack of masculine parental authority which makes enforcement of discipline within the family difficult; the traditional lack of savings- and capital-accumulation habits; and the folk belief that 'white is right,' which leads to a dependence upon the initiative of the white man. Personal indolence and laziness are sternly deprecated. Habits of hard work and thrift are extolled." [16] So long as these were seen as the standards of domineering whites, deep unconscious if not conscious forces stood in the way of their acceptance. This latent function of the Black Muslim movement may be supported by other latent functions—the learning of organizational skills, and an emphasis on education, for example. In the words of Essien-Udom, it provides a world "in which one can be black and unashamed." From a functional point of view, we might not be far from the truth to quote again Spindler's statement about the Peyote Cult, only changing the name of the group: Identification with the Black Muslims literally saves the self and gives it sanctions and directives for an integration of conflicting cultural patterns. This, at least, may be the result for some.

But we have said that an attacking sect is soon constrained by the society which it attacks, or it is changed by its own inner development, or both. I think it can be confidently foreseen that the Black Muslim movement will become more accommodative, devaluing the worldly success which it now emphasizes or calling for quiet reform; or it will shift over to culturally more acceptable modes of protest—political and economic; or it will die out. Those members who find life less humiliating and filled with more promise will not want to continue to identify with a group that attacks society too vehemently. That would endanger newly won self-respect and a more meaningful social status. Those who continue to find their lives filled with humiliation and frustration may lead the sect in a more violent direction, thus calling down repressive measures. Others in this situation will desert the group for its failure to save them and will join a new group with its promising but untested formula for salvation.

Thus the almost certain transformation of the Black Muslims does not mean the end of vigorous and even violent protest movements, often of a religious nature, among American Negroes. So long as serious disprivilege exists in the context of aroused aspirations, we can expect a succession of such movements. In fact, even economic success and occupational advancement, if they are unaccompanied by a reduction in the soul-searing effects of racial prejudice, will scarcely reduce the alienation that many Negroes feel toward society and the established religious patterns. For many today, the search for salvation is taking the form, not of sectarian protests within Christianity or of drastically new religious expressions, but of secular substitutes far removed from the major religious traditions.

Perhaps this development can be illustrated by a brief reference to the "black bourgeoisie," described so critically by Frazier. These are the middle- and upper-class Negroes who have hope, at least for individual economic and occupational success, but few of the disciplines necessary to take part in a religious or secular movement that struggles with their deeper problems. They still feel isolated, despite their relative economic success, from the society of which they are a part. The discrepancy between their economic standing and their social status is especially galling. They are too sophisticated to accept the extreme otherworldliness of most Negro sects or the "this-worldly escapism" of the Muslims. They are too alienated from the white world, which refuses to accept them even after they have won some of the measures of success, to embrace its religious perspectives. And their accomplishments, having been won for the most part on an individualistic basis, give them no sense of a shared fate from which a group protest might arise. They illustrate a paradox often found in religious matters: they are too well off to believe that they can afford a really demanding religion. Among the lower classes, religion often demands a major share of time and money. No easy religion would seem adequate in face of problems so deep as theirs. The black bourgeoisie, however, are receptive only to an easy religious substitute. Their search for salvation takes the form of relentless pursuit of recreation and pleasure. Out of that they hope to wring some meaning or at least to escape the crushing impact of segregation. Frazier describes the search for excitement and pleasure in terms that make it seem to be the middle-class equivalent of the search for toughness on the part of the lower-class gang members. Much of this activity centers around poker, which has become much more than a game or a way of winning money. It is a way of enhancing self-esteem, Frazier remarks, through overcoming fate. "In fact, poker is more than a form of recreation; it is the one absorbing interest of Negro 'society.' . . . The role of poker as a 'religious' force in the lives of the black bourgeoisie can not be discounted." [17]

Even in so brief a commentary as this we cannot disregard another religious movement among Negroes which is significantly different from the secular and religious responses to disprivilege we have discussed so far. Beginning, perhaps, with the "race churches" of the 1930's—those churches in the Northern cities that began to join the protest movement among Negroes—on to the Montgomery Improvement Association (organized at first to obtain the desegregation of the buses in Montgomery, Alabama, but growing to larger purposes) to the sit-in movement, and, most recently, to the freedom riders, there has been a succession of protests that are close to classic Christian sectarianism. Some of these developments are carried forward by groups not explicitly religious in organization, and are doubtless supported by some persons who interpret their actions in nonreligious terms. But there is little doubt that religious influences have been important. In terms of the four types which we described above, the sit-in and freedom-rider style of protest is characteristic of persons who have both the discipline necessary to plan and to suffer and the hope that they can struggle with their deepest problems without escaping or denying the society around them. They believe that the search for salvation need not involve a sharp attack on society and its dominant religion, but only on practices and institutions that are considered to be distortions of the society's basic values.

Who, in a disprivileged minority, will act on the basis

of such a belief? I would stress here the subtle interaction of a religious tradition and a social environment. A religious tradition that has encouraged passive adaptation, but has seeds of criticism within it, becomes something new in the minds of those who are aware of the changes in American society in the last generation, have come in contact with or heard about white persons religiously motivated to eliminate racial discrimination, have begun to climb the educational and occupational ladders, and are encouraged, by religious leaders sensitive to these developments, to reformulate their interpretations of life. In this context, we are not surprised to find a protesting sectarian movement similar to many others that have preceded it in Christendom.

V. Conclusion

What can we expect in the future? Will continued alienation from self and society support the growth of religious substitutes, from gangs to poker? Will we see a succession of movements akin in sociological meaning, if not in symbolism, to the Black Muslims? Or will we see a growth in the disciplined protests of the freedom riders, developing perhaps into an established sect, if our formula for this transformation, given above, is correct? The answer to these questions lies, of course, not only in the balance of the functions and dysfunctions of these various movements for the individuals involved and for society. It lies also in the course of development of American society. If we want more gangs or more Black Muslims, we certainly know how to create them; the procedure lies before us in the record of the last several decades. We also can see how to stimulate the growth of the somewhat more traditional Christian sectarian protests. The one thing we cannot do is to eliminate all of these movements, for they represent the range of endeavor among disprivileged persons to wring some dignity and meaning from life.

FOOTNOTES

1. Worsley, Peter. *The Trumpet Shall Sound. A Study of "Cargo" Cults in Melanesia.* London: MacGibbon and Kee, 1957, p. 44.
2. See Anthony Wallace, "Revitalization Movements," *American Anthropologist,* April, 1956, vol. 58, pp. 264-279.
3. Worsley, *op. cit.,* pp. 20-21.
4. Lesser, Alexander. "Cultural Significance of the Ghost Dance," *American Anthropologist,* Jan.-March, 1933, pp. 108-115.
5. Cohn, Werner. "Jehovah's Witnesses as a Proletarian Movement," *The American Scholar,* Summer, 1955, vol. 24, pp. 281-298.
6. Pike, Royston. *Jehovah's Witnesses.* New York: Philosophical Library, 1954, p. 136.
7. Lincoln, C. Eric. *The Black Muslims in America.* Boston: The Beacon Press, 1961, pp. 108-109.
8. Voget, Fred. "The American Indian in Transition: Reformation and Status Innovations," *American Journal of Sociology,* Jan., 1957, vol. LXII, pp. 371-372.
9. *Ibid.,* p. 374; see also Merle Deardoff, *The Religion of Handsome Lake,* Smithsonian Institution, Bureau of American Ethnology, Bulletin 149, 1951.
10. Spindler, George. "Personality and Peyotism in Menomini Indian Acculturation," *Psychiatry,* 1952, vol. 15, p. 155.
11. Voget, *op. cit.,* p. 374.
12. Niebuhr, H. Richard. *The Social Sources of Denominationalism.* New York: Henry Holt & Co., Inc., 1929, p. 67.
13. See Benton Johnson, "A Critical Appraisal of the Church-Sect Typology," *American Sociological Review,* Feb., 1957, vol. 22, pp. 88-92.
14. Yinger, J. Milton. "Contraculture and Subculture," *American Sociological Review,* Oct., 1960, vol. 25, pp. 625-635.
15. Rohrer, John H. and Edmonson, Munro S., eds. *The Eighth Generation. Cultures and Personalities of New Orleans Negroes.* New York: Harper & Brothers, 1960, p. 160.
16. Essien-Udom, E. U. *Black Nationalism. A Search for Identity in America.* Chicago: University of Chicago Press, 1962, pp. 14-15.
17. Frazier, E. Franklin. *Black Bourgeoisie.* Glencoe: The Free Press, 1957, pp. 211-212.

3

Religion and Social Change (*cont.*): Problems of Integration and Pluralism Among the Privileged

FOR THE first time in human history there are societies within which poverty—a shortage of basic goods and services—is no longer a central fact. Patterns of distribution leave some persons, perhaps even many persons, in poverty in the new affluent societies; but a larger number find themselves in relative comfort. Concomitant changes include the reduction of illness and the lengthening of life, a great increase in mobility, growth of leisure time, increased education, and the extension of contact across group lines. At the same time, many persons in these societies are concerned about loneliness in a sea of acquaintances, meaninglessness in a world of colliding values, self-alienation in a context of contradictory role requirements, and persistently awkward and tense interpersonal and intergroup relations. Illness and premature death, basic subsistence, lack of a position of minimum dignity—primordial problems that still loom large for most of mankind and for the disprivileged in the wealthy societies—are pushed into the background of experience. Some of the "ultimate questions" with which men struggle religiously spring from the universal human condition— man's finite quality, his capacity for self-centeredness, the tension between his ability to envisage "the fair city" and his inability to travel very far toward it. But closely related to these questions are others that relate to particular societies and particular conditions. And to those who struggle with these latter questions, they seem no less ultimate, no less religious, than those which are universal to man.

Think for a moment how changes in the population facts have affected the context of religion in the last two centuries. Life expectancy at birth in mid-eighteenth century was twenty-five years. In France, for example, Jean Fourastié reminds us, 430 to 440 out of 1,000 lived to marriage age. Half of the marriages reached their fifteenth anniversary. At fourteen years of age, the average child experienced the death of a parent. He was one of five children only half of whom lived to see their fifteenth birthday. Later, as the father of five children, he saw two or three die before his own death, at age fifty-two. He had survived two or three famines, long periods of serious food shortage, and several epidemics that cut down large numbers of persons in his community. "In former times death was in the midst of life as the cemetery is in the middle of the village. Since then, death, poverty, and suffering are retreating." [1]

It is important to remember how recently this situation has changed. The picture I have just drawn is not significantly different from the experience of man from time immemorial—perhaps only slightly more favorable. It is, in fact, not far from the experience of a large part of the human race today, something it is well for us to keep in mind in any attempt to understand religious and political movements. But for persons in the technologically advanced societies, there has been a revolutionary transformation. Life expectancy at birth is seventy years, not twenty-five. The average person is forty-two, not fourteen, when his first parent dies. Where formerly both parents were dead when the youngest child of a family reached maturity, it is now true that the normal couple lives fifteen years after the marriage of their youngest child.

I use these data only to say: the context within which religion is shaped has been suddenly transformed in the affluent societies. If, with Reinhold Niebuhr, we define religion as "a citadel of hope built on the edge of despair," we must note that the despair springs from a somewhat different series of tragedies and frustrations from those that have characterized human experience from the beginning, including, of course, the period when the major religious traditions were shaped. At this point, the conservative says that none of the ultimate questions is changed in the least; the basic religious quest, therefore, can only be confused by attention to local and temporal variations in the human condition. It is a mistake, I would agree, to exaggerate the change, for many of life's great problems remain. But it is equally a mistake to disregard the significantly different experiences of life in the urban, industrial society. With respect to some of the great issues around which much of religious belief and ritual have revolved for as far back as our records and imaginations can take us, there has been more change in the last two hundred years than in all the preceding life of man. It would be folly to doubt that this will have, and is having, enormous religious consequences.

I. Secularization or Religious Change?

Against the background of change briefly sketched in the introduction I would like to discuss two religious trends among the privileged members of modern societies, with special reference to the United States. Many interpreters have spoken of the growing interest in religion in the very context of apparent secularization. More recently there has been increasing discussion of religious separatism in the very context of ecumenicity. Not surprisingly, both of these trends have been interpreted as paradoxes. It is not always clear, however, which of the various meanings of the word "paradox" is intended. Perhaps most frequently the religious developments are believed to be paradoxical in the sense of a phenomenon with contradictory qualities. But underneath this common meaning of the word, a second connotation often appears: Contemporary religious developments are paradoxical because they are unexpected, difficult to explain, and contrary to received opinion.

I will spend only a little time stating the paradox in the first sense—the existence of contradictory trends—because this has been carefully examined by many persons. I shall only ask: Are the trends as contradictory as they appear? With respect to the second paradoxical quality of current religious events, we shall study somewhat more carefully this question: Are they actually surprising and contrary to what we might expect from knowledge of social trends and theories of the relationship of religion and society?

We noted in Chapter One that in the last twenty-five years there has been a strong increase in religious activity and interest in the judgment of most observers.[2] I will not ask whether or not the changes "really" represent religious developments, for the asking of such a question usually implies a substantive definition of religion that is too narrow for our purposes. (Only particular beliefs and practices—usually highly traditional ones—are defined as religious. One can then explain away all other developments—happily or unhappily—as merely pseudo-religious.) There have always been strong religious forces in the United States, of course, and events of the last few decades partly signify a revival of an interest that had lagged between 1900 and 1940, to pick two arbitrary dates. Yet some aspects of the contemporary situation are new. Although a Supreme Court decision in June, 1962, outlawed the reading of a prayer officially designated by the Regents of the State of New York for use in public schools, this only slightly qualifies the fact that local, state, and national political processes have steadily acquired more religious symbols and practices. Berger has recently argued that religion has become so deeply embedded in American society that we have to think in terms of an establishment, in a nontechnical sense of the word.[3] And Lenski found, contrary to widely held views concerning the influence of the city and of "Americanization," that the most urbanized and most Americanized segments of the Detroit area population were the strongest supporters of the churches for most groups.[4]

Despite such evidences of growing support for churches and strengthened interest in religious questions, American society is often described as highly secularized. It is not entirely clear, however, what secularization means. There is some tendency to make it synonymous with a decline in orthodoxy or a reduction in the acceptance of traditional beliefs. In such a definition secularization becomes synonymous with religious change. Herberg, in his influential study, notes that over four-fifths of adult Americans accept the Bible as the revealed word of God, yet seldom read it and know little of its content. ". . . The religion which actually prevails among Americans today has lost much of its authentic Christian (or Jewish) content. Even when they are thinking, feeling, or acting religiously, their thinking, feeling, and acting do not bear an unequivocal relation to the faiths they profess. Americans think, feel, and act in terms quite obviously secularist at the very time that they exhibit every sign of a widespread religious revival."[5]

In this statement, Professor Herberg implies a standard definition of the concept of secularization—the separation of religious motives, feelings, and decisions from other aspects of life; but he also suggests another meaning— persons acting religiously in a way that does not express directly the faith they profess. These two processes are not the same; and I believe it is a mistake to use the same term with reference to them. It is one thing to have many

of life's decisions carried out without reference to religion
—the usual dictionary meaning of secularization. It is
another thing to redefine one's religion while disguising
or obscuring the process by holding, somewhat super-
ficially, to many of the symbols of the earlier religious
system. Religious change is usually a latent process, carried
on beneath symbols of nonchange. Only if one defines
religion statically—the received beliefs and practices are
religious, departures from them are not—is it meaningful
to think of religious change as secularization. Herberg does
not define religion statically. His double meaning of the
term "secularization" derives, I believe, from the fact that
he is unhappy about the religious trends—the decline
of "authentic Christian (or Jewish) content," and the
rise of humanistic and nationalistic themes. He is not
quite ready to call the current developments religion; yet
his analysis leads him to the conclusion that they are.
He resolved the dilemma by using the word "secularization" in two ways, referring on the one hand to
religious movements that lack "authenticity" and on the
other to the application of nonreligious standards to life.

Peter Berger shows the same dual meaning for the
concept of secularization in his interesting book, *The
Noise of Solemn Assemblies*. Religious motives, he suggests, are segregated within the religious institution in
contemporary America; they are thought to be of little
relevance to other aspects of life. Despite the current attention to religion, it scarcely affects the course of the
revolutionary developments of the day—urbanization, the
transformation of the sexual ethic, business and political
processes. Professor Berger then proceeds, however, to
describe the ways religion in America today supports
American institutions and values. The churches aid the
search for "social adjustment" (the pressures to submerge
one's own views, to be a "regular guy," to avoid the "dark
side of life"). Religion has become so closely related to
our political institutions and processes that Berger be-

lieves, as we have noted, that we should speak in terms of an establishment—not, of course, in the legal or technical sense, but in the sense of strong mutual involvement of our religious beliefs with our political processes and institutions.

Perhaps Berger's thesis can be summed up in his phrase that religion affirms "the O.K. World." It supports the dominant values and institutions of society.

I wonder if it is not a mistake to think of such "churchlike" behavior as irrelevant. It is highly relevant to the process of supporting the basic institutions and values of the society. What Berger, Herberg, and others are saying is that the church has too little relevance for the "prophetic task" of reforming the world. America is highly "secular," in their view, because there is so little tension between the prevailing religious institutions and the secular order. This is the ancient prophetic cry that the church has lost its vision; it has been conquered by society and is useful for little more than sanctifying the social order with its weaknesses and injustices. I do not object to this value declaration in the least—indeed I share a great deal of the view that there ought to be sustantial tension between religion and society and nation. Such a view ought not to be used, however, to obscure our analysis of the fact that the churches of those who are comfortable in a society are almost always well accommodated to that society. This is not secularization. It is instead one of the most persistent functions of religion—whether we applaud or lament the fact. Those of us who share sectarian religious tendencies—who want religion to stand in constructive tension with society—need to keep our values fully in view when we speak of secularization. It would not be at all easy to demonstrate that Christianity in 1900 or 1850 or 1800 was more "universal," less bound by class and nation in America than it is today. The church, as contrasted with the sect, works within the structure of the established social order. What is often called secularization today is the inevitable adjustment of the church to dramatic changes in the world within which it works.

Religious research and analysis would be better served by distinguishing clearly between secularization and religious change. If we do so, we will observe, I believe, that American society is not highly secularized. The religious "boom" of the last quarter of a century is not a superficial phenomenon that hides much stronger tendencies toward religious decline. It is just as "authentic," just as "genuine" a religious development as a revival of more traditional beliefs would be. What we are witnessing is the development of new religious forms. The life conditions of the middle and upper classes in our urban societies, so dramatically different from anything mankind has ever before experienced, are having significant religious consequences. The changes are being obscured by the continuity of symbols; they are, quite understandably, opposed by most religious professionals—with the result that much of the new religion is developing at the hands of laymen—but the changes continue nevertheless.

To say that the increasing identity with churches alongside the growth of nontraditional symbols and forms is a religious movement, not secularization, is not to say that one applauds the course of events. I am simply recording the fact that American religious perspectives are changing as society changes. This is precisely what we would expect, among the privileged as well as the disprivileged, from sociological theory of "the church." The alternative to the development of a "cultural religion," as it is often called—a religion that supports and interacts fairly harmoniously with the values and institutions of the society—is not the triumph of some prophetic message, bringing full justice to society. The alternative is some quasi religion that attempts to perform the function of lending legitimacy to the values of the society. It is well to remember that such a substitute, an openly nationalistic movement, for example, would develop largely in separation from the sectarian dimension of religion that helps to prevent such thorough sanctification of the *status quo* that the dynamic adjustments vital to a changing society are blocked.

If one defines religion statically—in terms of a system of beliefs and practices that emerged at a given time and were subject thereafter to no *essential* revision—religious change is nearly identical with secularization. It represents the falling away from the great tradition. If one thinks of religion, however, as an ongoing search, subject to changed forms and revised myths, then lack of orthodoxy does not mean the weakening of religion. It can be a sign of strength.

In short, the increase in religious activity and interest in the very context of supposed "secularization" is paradoxical only to the sectarian, not to the analyst. It is an indication of an expected *churchlike* response to dramatic changes in the conditions of life among the middle and upper classes in a prosperous society. The changes have been fundamental and rapid, as social changes go. One would expect a revived and new religious movement to develop in an effort to struggle with the new aspects of the problems of group cohesion and individual salvation.

As I have stated, the permanent problems of the human condition remain, so that the new are heaped upon the old, creating a complex religious situation. The catastrophic wars of the last few generations, the vast cruelties of totalitarian governments, the incredible threats of future war make it apparent to even the most insensitive of us that man has won no salvation from premature death, injustice, and the capacity for hostility. These developments also support the religious revival, but less strongly among the laymen in the United States than among religious professionals. Theologians, made sensitive to these tragedies by their heritage, have seen in them a confirmation of their orthodox views. This same heritage has made them less sensitive to the new crises of affluence, mobility, and anomie. If the new religious boom seems shallow in intellectual content, poor in symbolism, and lacking in universality, it may be largely because the religious leaders who might overcome these weaknesses are not at home in the urban world and ill equipped by their traditional views to grapple with many of the contemporary religious issues.

II. *Integration or Pluralism?*

Many observers of the American scene speak of another paradox. There are strong pressures toward cultural unity, expressing themselves religiously in the form of denominational mergers, interdenominational councils and cooperation, and other ecumenical activities. At the same time there remain at least three distinctive religious structures which support many separate influences. There is a tendency for Protestants, Catholics, and Jews to live in separate neighborhoods, to belong to separate associations of various kinds, and to insist strongly on intrafaith marriage.

We shall ask if both of these at least partially conflicting things are true. If so, are they paradoxical not only in the sense of a phenomenon with contradictory qualities, but also in the sense of being contrary to what one would expect on the basis of accepted ideas concerning the relationship of religion and society?

In the discussion we should keep in mind that there are conflicting values as well as conflicting trends. On the one hand, our tradition of pluralism supports the desirability of separate religious groups. They are believed to be a source of strength for a democratic society—expressive of individual freedom and a protection against an overly close identity between religion and nation. On the other hand, religious diversity can be a source of conflict. Carried to great lengths it produces "parallel columns" of social organization that divide a society into intolerant subsocieties incapable of the cooperation and compromise necessary for social harmony.

Lee has summarized in a very helpful manner the wide variety of ways in which the movement toward church unity is expressing itself in the United States. It is taking place in the context of such unifying secular developments as these: the reduction of differences between country and city, the decline of sectionalism, racial desegregation, the compressing of our stratification pyramid, the lessening of the sense of ethnic differences with the sharp reduction of immigration, and the growth of a more completely shared culture as a result of the national communication networks and mobility. Reversing Richard Niebuhr's thesis that sectional, ethnic, class, and racial differences were among the important "social sources of denomination-alism," Lee argues that these unifying trends in American society are social sources of ecumenicalism. The variety of ways in which church unity is being expressed is wide: The National Council of Churches, mergers of denominations, local community churches, coordination of activities on college campuses, the use of common literature, and the development of a "common-core Protestantism" are among the most important expressions of unity.[6]

It is readily apparent that the trend toward unity encompasses little outside Protestantism. Even within Protestantism, Lee notes that there are some tendencies toward heightened denominationalism, a continuing separate group of sects, a vigorously anti-unity fundamentalist movement, and the largely separate Southern Baptist Convention. Much of the resistance to ecumenicalism found in these forces can be explained by the continued operation of secular influences that divide on the basis of class, race, and region.

The same explanation—continuing secular differences—is less helpful, however, in explaining the separation of Catholics, Protestants, and Jews, among whom only small evidences of cooperation are found. Secular differences of

class, occupation, educational level, and the like have
declined. There is no reason, in principle, to expect the
social pressures toward unity and ecumenicity to stop at
the point where the deeper lines of cleavage have run—
the lines between Protestants, Catholics, and Jews. To be
sure, one would expect more and longer-lasting forces toward secular similarity and unity to be needed to bridge
these deeper and historically more significant lines of
cleavage. The direction of change, however, should be the
same if secular differences among the major religious
groups are declining. Most evidence suggests that the social
sources of religious divisions are declining; yet separation
remains, in the judgment of many persons, as sharp as
ever. Coleman describes these seemingly contrary forces
well:

> The economic, ethnic, and other groups which have paralleled
> religious groupings in the past are coming to cross-cut them now:
> Catholics have diffused upwards in the economic structure, and
> outward geographically to the suburbs; Jews similarly are less con-
> centrated in particular economic roles and geographic locations
> than before; Protestants who grew up in one sect in a community
> are dispersed and recongregated in communities where sects must
> combine to survive. In sum, economic and geographic mobility is
> imposing new conditions of association and group identification
> on persons of different religious groups. These conditions will not
> break down religious cleavages; to the contrary, they may some-
> times thrust together in a single community a combination of
> religious groups which makes for conflict; yet this dispersion has
> its effect in many ways; certainly by increasing the possibilities of
> cross-pressure; perhaps by bringing religious conflict more often
> to the community level, less often to the national or state level;
> perhaps by reducing intergroup suspicion and hostility which feed
> on disassociation; perhaps by initial disputes followed by gradual
> reduction of tensions. Little is known about such effects; much
> could be learned by research on communities faced with influx
> from a different religious group.[7]

All of the consequences mentioned by Coleman seem
plausible, particularly in the short run. But in the long

run, one would expect that those forces producing secular similarities would also tend to reduce religious conflict, produce more similar religious values and forms, promote interreligious cooperation, break up the solidarity of communal religious structures, and increase the rate of intermarriage across religious lines.

An important corollary to this statement should be mentioned, although I will not explore it here. Forces promoting social similarities between the unchurched (often called the "secularists") and church members might be expected to promote communication and cooperation between them. Again, on the surface at least, there are few signs of such developments. The ecumenical movement, for example, which is primarily a Protestant movement, not only has not done much to close the gap between Protestant and Catholic, but it excludes liberal Protestants for their various heresies—although this word, of course, is not used—and has only slight connection with those unchurched individuals and groups who may share many of the values of the ecumenicalists. It would be my guess that insofar as those who support the ecumenical trend and those who are unchurched are alike in class, region of the country, educational level, and in other social ways there will be an increasing amount of interaction between them. (I would add that this seems to me to be a vitally necessary development.)

To return to the question of interaction across religious lines in the United States, we must observe that most students of the situation believe that the distinctiveness of the three subcommunities has scarcely been modified. Among many others, Kennedy, Herberg, and most recently Lenski have emphasized the extent to which Protestants, Catholics, and Jews remain separate in American society despite the sharp reduction of differences among them on many secular grounds. Ethnic, class, and regional differences *within* these three groups have been reduced; barriers to interaction, cooperation, and intermarriage be-

tween Irish Catholic and Italian Catholic, German Jew
and Russian Jew, English Protestant and Swedish Protestant have been reduced. But the three major groups remain distinctive. In Kennedy's well known phrase, America
has developed not a single, but a triple melting pot.[8] The
degree of separation is nowhere nearly as great as that
shown by the "columns" of Catholic, Protestant, and
humanist in the Netherlands, where separation by residence, education, and work situation is the rule.[9] Nor does
the United States look like Austria, where the division
into Socialist, Nationalist, and Christian-Social Conservative *Lager* has sharply split the society for decades.[10] Yet
there are clear evidences of separation in the United
States. Lenski wisely notes that we must distinguish the
associational (church membership) aspects of religious
groups from the communal aspects (family, friends, and
neighborhood interaction). One may remain strong while
the other declines. Thus Jews have weak associational but
strong communal ties with one another. Catholics have
strong associational ties, indicated by regular church at-
tendance and widespread acceptance of Catholic doctrines.
Their communal ties are of medium strength. The family
is a strong religious unit, but there is some intermarriage,
and Catholics have many non-Catholic friends. Although
neighborhoods are not religiously homogeneous, there is a
strong tendency toward religious clustering in the city and
its suburbs. Protestants demonstrate medium strength of
both associational and communal ties. Although he recognizes the various tendencies, Lenski summarizes the
situation by referring to "our current drift toward a 'compartmentalized society.' " [11]

Although such data seem to challenge the principle of
the social sources of church unity (secular differences between Protestants, Catholics, and Jews having been reduced), they may instead simply point to the offsetting
influence of other principles. In a mobile and rapidly
changing world, we cling rather tightly to our religious

subcommunity as one of the few points of stability. Even in less perilous times men hold tenaciously to their religious identity; for one does not lightly revise the way he has learned to deal with his ultimate problems. The strength of religious organizations supports these forces. It is clear, for example, that some aspects of the influence of the Roman Catholic Church are "anti-acculturative," as Spiro puts it. Through the parochial school and by other separating procedures, the Church isolates its children from some elements of the dominant culture; it organizes their lives around a somewhat different set of sacred symbols.[12] On the basis of his data from the Detroit area, Lenski holds that the distinctiveness of the Catholic subculture is not being reduced by the shift from immigrant to "old American" nor by status improvement. Middleclass Catholics of a third or earlier generation are in some ways more deeply involved in the partially separate community than are lower-class first- or second-generation Catholics.

This observation is difficult to interpret, however. In the country as a whole, if not in Detroit, "old American" Catholics are likely to be Irish. For the Irish, the Church was the rallying point for national opposition to England. Later migrants from Italy and Eastern Europe came from areas where the Church was identified more easily with an oppressive society than with a movement of liberation and national identity. Unless we control for national origin, therefore, observations about old and new Catholic migrants do not necessarily support the thesis of the continuing vitality of a separate Catholic tradition especially among the most "Americanized."

This qualification, however, scarcely removes the fact that a clearly distinctive Catholic tradition maintains a great deal of strength in the United States. To record this fact is neither to applaud nor to regret it. Judgments need to rest on an appraisal of all of the long-run consequences —a task of great proportions. Berger has recently suggested

that Protestants owe Catholics a debt of gratitude for
having maintained a stronger tension between their religious perspective and the secular world than have Protestants. Many of his fellow Protestants are likely to reply
that unfortunately that tension includes opposition to
the secular tradition of civil liberties, less regard for the
principle of tolerance, and the support of other values
that stand in opposition to both democracy and the
Protestant view of the world. I am interested, not in exploring the controversy here, but only in noting that somewhat separate religious communities persist.

There need to be made, however, two modifications of
this description of America's distinct religious groups. In
the first place, such differences as exist are still to be explained, to an important degree, not as existing in spite
of drastic reduction of secular differences but because of
the continuation of significant secular differences. Were
one to revise the late Richard Niebuhr's classic study, first
published in 1929, he would find no shortage of material
to document "the social sources of denominationalism."
There are still regional, class, rural-urban, occupational,
educational, and ethnic differences among the major religious groups. Prejudice still produces group cohesion.
The arrival of large numbers of Catholics and Jews at the
third generation in America is not the end of a process of
change; it is the beginning of a new situation in which
memories of one's grandparents mingle with contemporary experiences.

In a highly mobile and changing society, indicators
of social status are capricious and unreliable, a fact that
encourages some persons to cling tightly to such indicators as are available. This tendency creates one of the
strongest obstacles to racial desegregation of neighborhoods, because residential area and house have to substitute for the family connection that marks status in a
stable society. The same influence creates barriers to unity
among churches on the local level. One's church in the

United States is an important, although not infallible, status indicator. Lee observes that mergers are usually between churches that draw from the same class range; and Underwood found that Catholic churches in "Paper City" were more class segregated than the Protestant churches.[13] On the national level, interdenominational and interfaith cooperation is strongly affected by the class system, lending support to Berger's statement: "Not only is this 'interfaith' solidarity functional in maintaining the social systems as it now exists, but it also has an ideological functon as well—namely, it serves to obscure the reality of class segregation. Having participated in the rhetorics of tolerance and mutual good will, one may now harbor the illusion that the social divisions of the society have been superseded by religious solidarity." [14]

Thus social forces continue to operate to preserve religious differentiation despite the reduction of some of the separating influences.

In the second place, there is something of a tendency among some writers to exaggerate the extent of separation among the three major religious groups, disregarding the evidence of cooperation and adjustment among them. Many economic, political, and educational associations cut across religious lines. And at least a few highly placed religious leaders are engaged in discussions concerned with the reduction of religious separation. (Confrontation and dialogue are words loaded with the connotations of this process.) I will discuss the evidence with respect to one aspect of the question only, interfaith marriage, which can well be considered the most sensitive index of the extent of separation across religious lines. The data, as is well known, are inadequate; but there has been sufficient improvement in the last few years that we can speak with a little confidence. Earlier studies of interfaith marriage tended to emphasize how infrequently it occurred and sometimes to project a trend into the future without any specification of the conditions that inhibit or promote intermarriage. Hollingshead, for example, in his study of a sample of all marriages performed in New Haven in 1948 found that 25.6 percent of Protestants, 6.2 percent of Catholics, and 2.9 percent of Jews had married outside their religious group. He then observes: "From the viewpoint of assimilation, marriages across religious lines are crucial if the triple melting-pot is to become a single melting-pot. But as Kennedy's and our data show, we are going to have three pots boiling merrily side by side with little fusion between them for an indefinite period." [15] It is difficult to see how he arrived at this prediction with the data in hand. What would be required to make such a prediction meaningful is a careful specification of previous rates and a study of trends in those social forces believed to be related to the extent of intermarriage.

Kennedy's study, cited by Hollingshead, recorded an increase in religious intermarriage in New Haven, between 1870 and 1940, from 5 to 16 percent among Catholics, from 1 to 20 percent among Protestants, and from 0 to 6 percent among Jews. Although Hollingshead found that the rates for Catholics and Jews were lower in 1948 than in 1940, in her study of the 1950 records, Kennedy found intermarriage rates of 30 percent, 27 percent, and 4 percent for Protestants, Catholics, and Jews. These data certainly do not support the statement that there will be little fusion for an indefinite period. We need to ask: What is the effect of the proportion of persons of a given religious group in a society or a community on its rate of interfaith marriage? What happens when economic, educational, and occupational differences among religious groups are reduced? How is the intensity of identification with a particular church, or the degree of orthodoxy of belief, involved? How does prejudice affect the rate of intermarriage? If the intermarriage rate goes up or down, does this mean a change in personal inclination or the recommendations of religious leaders, or does it reflect a change in the extent of housing segregation based on religion, so that more or fewer young persons of different religious training meet?

Keeping such questions in mind, we can begin to hazard a guess about the extent to which religion today enters into marriage decisions and the likelihood that it will tomorrow. The special United States Census study of religion in 1957 found that 21.6 percent of Catholics were married to non-Catholics; 8.6 percent of Protestants were married to non-Protestants; and 7.2 percent of Jews were married to persons outside their group. Taking his data from the *Catholic Directory*, Thomas found that almost 30 percent of marriages involving a Catholic were mixed. This included only sanctioned Catholic marriages; were nonsanctioned included, the rate would be higher.[16] Simply to take these figures without examination is probably to underestimate the extent of interfaith marriage. Even if religion played no part whatsoever in marriage choice, approximately 70 percent of Protestant, 25 percent of Catholic, and 4 percent of Jewish marriages would be *intra*faith. For the country as a whole, this means that about 55 percent of all marriages would be intrafaith and 45 percent interfaith if the religious beliefs of partners were a matter of pure chance. The 1957 census sample found that approximately 12 percent of the marriages were in fact across religious lines at the time of the census. In other words, over a quarter of the "possible" interfaith marriages occurred.

These data, in fact, probably seriously underestimate the intermarriage rate since they do not take into account the effects of change of religion by one or both partners after marriage. If information from one community is a guide, it is important to distinguish between interfaith marriage at the time of the wedding and later. Lenski reports that for the Detroit area sample, 32 percent of the white Protestants and Catholics had married outside their religious group. Only 15 percent, however, indicated that at the time of the interview their marriage partner was of a different faith. Conversion of one partner to the religion of the other was thus common, although we have no knowledge of the strength of the new church identity. We are greatly in need of study of the religious and other consequences of such intrafamily conversion.

There is another reason why the census figures may tend to exaggerate the extent to which religion enters into marriage decisions: they are based on national data that disregard regional, class, educational, and racial differences which affect the results. Tabulate Negro Protestants and white Protestants separately, and the interfaith marriage rate of the white Protestants is seen to be significantly higher than the total Protestant rate. Negro Protestants doubtless have a low rate of religious exogamy, although I know of no data on this question, because there are relatively few colored persons in other religious groups. Assuming that most persons from the South marry persons from the South, we get a high rate of intrafaith marriage regardless of any influence of religious motives, because of the relative religious homogeneity of the region.

In his study of midtown Manhattan, based on an area-probability sample, Heiss found that 21.4 percent of Catholics were intermarried, 33.9 percent of Protestants, and 18.4 percent of Jews.[17] Although one cannot generalize to other areas from these data, they may indicate what takes place when the three religious groups live in quite close proximity. Among these three groups, 25 percent were intermarried. On sheer chance grounds—that is, if no religious factors were involved—59 percent would have intermarried. To put this in other terms, out of one hundred interfaith marriages that might have occurred, forty-two did occur, and this despite the possible inhibiting effects of differences in race, class, age and sex distribution, and specific neighborhood.

Regarding Jewish exogamy, which is generally the lowest among the three major religious bodies in the United States, Rosenthal reports percentages, for various years from 1953 to 1959, of 11.5 in Washington, 31 in Iowa, 17.2 in San Francisco, and 20 and 37 for two counties in the San Francisco area.[18] These data may give further support to the hypothesis that members of a group are more likely to intermarry, other things being equal, when they make up a small proportion of a community rather than a large proportion.

In the absence of good comparative data for the United States which could indicate changes through time, information from Canada is of value. Between 1927 and 1957, rates of religious exogamy doubled, from 5.8 percent to 11.5 percent. The percentage increase among Protestants was from 5.0 to 11.6, for Catholics from 7.2 to 11.5, and for Jews from 3.0 to 6.8. Intermarriage rates are lowest for a group where it makes up a large proportion of the population of a province. The reduction of association between ethnic group, class, and religion is doubtless involved in the increased rate.[19] Since the Canadian rate in 1957 is almost identical with the rate of interfaith marriage found in the special census in the United States in 1957, it is tempting to assume that the pattern of change since 1927 has been about the same; but the societies are sufficiently different to make that anything more than a guess.

I have cited these data not to demonstrate that religious exogamy is either frequent or infrequent, but to try to get as accurate a picture as possible. In my judgment the rate of interfaith marriage is higher than is usually noted and the forces that seem to increase it are growing stronger. But the more important question relates to its various consequences. Here our information is even less good. In the many studies of marital success and happiness, for example, there is a tendency to compare the religiously intermarried with the intramarried without attention to other possible differences between them. To say that interfaith marriages have a higher rate of divorce is not to indicate what the causes are. The appropriate question is:

Would these same people have had greater success had they married within their religious group? We cannot know this, but we can try to compare them with other-wise equivalent persons who have married within their religious group. Only when two groups similar in class, educational level, urbanness, degree of religious fervor and other personality measures are compared can any observed differences in marital happiness or success be related to religious endogamy or exogamy. Lacking such controlled comparisons, we are left an open field for the operation of value judgments in the research process. I do not imply by this that religious difference is unimportant in marriage. There are grounds for expecting it to be associated with some problems. But research that fails to eliminate the influence of other factors cannot explore the question adequately.

The possible consequences of interfaith marriage for religion are equally important. It is the marginal member of a religious group, not the strongly identified member, who is most likely to intermarry. This may swell the ranks of the unchurched, if casual member marries casual mem-ber, with neither interested in taking the lead. It may, however, lead to new religious identities, if the partners move together into new interests. Or it may lead to the conversion of the less concerned partner to the faith of the more concerned. This too can have a chain of con-sequences as a group acquires as adults numbers of persons brought up in a different religious tradition. It is not im-possible that a broader ecumenicalism than we now can see might be given some reinforcement in a context of extensive interfaith marriage. Or new religious develop-ments, springing from a society where older identities were being obscured, might be promoted. These are only speculations on my part offered in the hope that they may help us to avoid the overly easy interpretations of the consequences of interfaith marriage.

And thus I can come back to the theme of this section

—the paradox of ecumenicity in the context of continuing religious separation. Both tendencies can certainly be found in the United States today. This makes analysis difficult; but study of social trends and social pressures by the methods of the sociology of religion makes both trends comprehensible. In this sense, there is no paradox.

FOOTNOTES

1. Fourastié, Jean. "Three Comments on the Near Future of Mankind," *Diogenes*, Winter, 1960, no. 32, pp. 1-16.
2. Douglass, Truman. "Ecological Changes and the Church," *Annals of the American Academy of Political and Social Science*, Nov., 1960, vol. 332, p. 81.
3. Berger, Peter. *The Noise of Solemn Assemblies.* Garden City: Doubleday & Company, Inc., 1961.
4. Lenski, Gerhard. *The Religious Factor. A Sociological Study of Religion's Impact on Politics, Economics, and Family Life.* Garden City: Doubleday & Company, Inc., 1961, pp. 39-50. For a contrary view, emphasizing the continuity of religious influence in the United States, see Seymour Lipset, "Religion in America: What Religious Revival?" *Columbia University Forum*, Winter, 1959.
5. Herberg, Will. *Protestant—Catholic—Jew.* Garden City: Doubleday & Company, Inc., 1955, p. 15. See also his papers on "Religion in a Secularized Society," *Review of Religious Research*, Spring, 1962, vol. 3, pp. 145-158 and Fall, 1962, vol. 4, pp. 33-45.
6. See Robert Lee, *The Social Sources of Church Unity*, New York: Abingdon Press, 1960.
7. Coleman, James S. "Social Cleavage and Religious Conflict," *Journal of Social Issues*, 1956, vol. 12, no. 3, pp. 47-48.
8. Kennedy, Ruby Jo. "Single or Triple Melting Pot? Intermarriage Trends in New Haven, 1870-1940," *American Journal of Sociology*, Jan., 1944, vol. 49, pp. 331-339; and "Single or Triple Melting Pot? Intermarriage in New Haven, 1870-1950," *American Journal of Sociology*, July, 1952, vol. 58, pp. 56-59.
9. Moberg, David. "Social Differentiation in the Netherlands," *Social Forces*, May, 1961, vol. 39, pp. 333-337.
10. Diamont, Alfred. *Austrian Catholics and the First Republic.* Princeton: Princeton University Press, 1960.

11. Lenski, *op. cit.*, chap. 2 and pp. 326-330.
12. Spiro, M. E. "The Acculturation of American Ethnic Groups," *American Anthropologist*, Dec., 1955, vol. 57, pp. 1240-1252.
13. Underwood, Kenneth. *Protestant and Catholic.* Boston: The Beacon Press, 1957.
14. Berger, *op. cit.*, p. 90.
15. Hollingshead, A. B. "Cultural Factors in the Selection of Marriage Mates," *American Sociological Review*, Oct., 1950, vol. 15, p. 624.
16. United States Bureau of the Census, "Religion Reported by the Civilian Population of the United States: March, 1957," *Current Population Reports*, Series P-20, No. 79, 1958; John L. Thomas, "The Factor of Religion in the Selection of Marriage Mates," *American Sociological Review*, Aug., 1951, vol. 16, pp. 487-491.
17. Heiss, Jerold. "Premarital Characteristics of the Religiously Intermarried in an Urban Area," *American Sociological Review*, Feb., 1960, vol. 25, pp. 47-55.
18. Rosenthal, Erich. "Acculturation Without Assimilation? The Jewish Community in Chicago, Illinois," *American Journal of Sociology*, Nov., 1960, vol. LXVI, pp. 275-288.
19. Heer, David. "The Trend of Interfaith Marriages in Canada: 1922-1957," *American Sociological Review*, April, 1962, vol. 27, pp. 245-250.

4

Religious Groups and Ethnic Groups: Social Forces Involved in Group Identification or Withdrawal

THE STUDY of religious groups and of individual feelings of attachment to them is strengthened by simultaneous study of other groups, because the rise in importance of one association is often accompanied by decline in the strength of identity with another. In a mobile society, sectional loyalties fade and national loyalties grow in strength. In an open society, where social mobility is common, few persons will think of themselves primarily in terms of class location; but if the channels of mobility are closed, one's class identity may become a crucial fact. This general principle can guide us in a more intensive investigation of one of the problems we discussed in the previous chapter: To what degree do contemporary Americans identify themselves with separate religious groups; is there much transfer of religious loyalty?

Our focus of attention in this chapter will be on internal processes within ethnic groups. The question of their continuation or disappearance becomes particularly interesting, and complicated, when reinforcing lines of identity are separated. It has often been true in the United States that one's national or ethnic origin was bound so closely to his religious affiliation that Irish-Catholic, Swedish-Lutheran, or Russian-Jew were descriptive of single identities to a great degree. Class and regional factors supported the complex unity. What happens when these connections are broken? In terms of the topic of this book, we are interested particularly in what happens to the religious aspect of these multiple identities when, as a result of "Americanization" and of geographical and social mobility, it is no longer bound to the others.

A generation ago it was widely believed that the many minority groups in American society would readily become acculturated to the dominant patterns and, in the course of a few generations, assimilated into the total population. Although racial groups were generally excepted from this thesis, its proponents contended that linguistic and national-origin lines would be obliterated and even religious divisions, unlikely to be eliminated in a society that practiced freedom of religion, would be greatly reduced. In recent years, this thesis has been challenged.[1] Many students of the current scene argue that the process of assimilation is neither inevitable nor desirable. Extensive acculturation can scarcely be denied, but assimilation—the loss of group identity—has become problematic, both as fact and as value.

Perhaps this issue can be explored most effectively, not by asserting one proposition or another, but by raising a series of questions: What are the conditions under which minority groups—ethnic, racial, or religious—persist as distinguishable entities within the structure of society? What conditions are associated with their dissolution? What are the consequences for society of the maintenance of groups on the basis of race, religion, or ethnicity, rather than, or in addition to, groups based on occupation, residence, class, avocational interests, or other criteria? It is well to remember that "group" is a generic term that includes collectivities of widely varying degrees of cohesiveness. It does not include statistical categories (all persons whose names begin with "S," for example), for the term implies as a minimum an awareness by the individuals involved of some common identity and shared fate. The members of more cohesive groups will, in addition, engage in social interaction. And if this interaction is persistent and repetitive, the group is characterized by social structure.[2] We can avoid errors of interpretation if we keep these levels of cohesiveness in mind in the study of minority groups. Even the simple awareness of a common identity may be an influence on minority-group members. But it is the meaning of "group" in the fuller sense, involving social interaction and social structure, that is of greatest importance.

To this sociological view we can profitably add the social-psychological concept of "reference group," by means of which we look at groups through the eyes of an individual. The term is not synonymous with a group to which one belongs, although membership groups are perhaps the most numerous and important reference groups. A group that one uses as his context of belief, motivation, and action with regard to a specific issue is his reference group. It may be used as a kind of checkpoint in making comparisons and contrasts; or it may be a group in which one wishes to hold or to gain membership— thus a group whose standards and claims are paramount in choice situations.[3]

The special study of minority groups and their religious expressions is best carried on by treating it as one phase of the general study of groups, seeking to answer such questions as these: What conditions promote group cohesiveness? What satisfactions come from groups? How do groups shape perception, motivation, and behavior? What happens when the different groups to which one belongs offer contradictory interpretations and influences? What processes are set in motion when social change or physical and social mobility weaken the group structures to which one has become accustomed?

I. Forces Influencing Identification
with Religious Groups

When these questions are asked with reference to minority groups, in an effort to discover the forces involved in group identification or withdrawal, we are led to many ambivalent situations and paradoxes. Apparent group pride and identity may mask self-alienation and low morale. The decline of distinctiveness in the standards of a group may be accompanied by an increase in the sense of identity with it. The forces at work on one generation—struggling with its particular problems of identity—are sometimes dramatically different from the forces influencing the next generation. The quick observer of this complicated situation is liable to mistake an eddy for the mainstream, a short-run trend for a permanent development.

With these hazards in mind, I am led to the belief, as I study racial, ethnic, and religious groups in America, that the assimilation thesis is neither as accurate as its proponents thought nor as wide of the mark as many current writers believe. Language differences have been reduced, but certainly not eliminated.[4] Most of the Indian tribes that were here when the Europeans came are still in existence as distinct groups with separate cultures. The continuing importance of foreign-born persons in the American population should not be forgotten. Although the percentage of foreign-born has fallen from the high point of 14.5 in 1910 to 5.8 in 1960, there are still over ten million persons in the United States who were born abroad. According to Donald Bogue's estimates, this number will increase slightly in the next twenty years.[5] Pride in national group has been tenacious with some people and has resulted in the continuation of separate associations, not simply among those with a low degree of acculturation, but sometimes among those who are thoroughly estab-

lished. On the basis of his study of Norwegians in Wisconsin, Munch writes: "In human society, there are forces
working both ways, both toward assimilation and toward
differentiation of groups. And the existence in this country
of easily distinguishable ethnic groups, even after more
than a hundred years' residence, through three or four or
even five generations, under a tremendous social pressure,
suggests that here there have been *positive* forces working
towards a *differentiation* of groups on the basis of ethnic
origin." [6]

Related to language and national origin, and probably
more important than either, are the lines of religious
division. Not only are there distinctions among the major
groups, but also internal patterns of differentiation. In
Protestantism, there have been tendencies toward union
among some churches, but national churches, especially
among the Lutherans, are still important. Although some
Roman Catholic Churches are multinational, many continue to have an ethnic identity. Judaism can be characterized as an ethnic church whose members are drawn
almost entirely from those of common descent; and its
internal differentiation reflects, although less and less
clearly, differences in national origin.

Ninety-five percent of Americans readily identify themselves with one of the major religious groups, approximately
two-thirds with Protestantism, one-quarter with Catholicism, and 3 percent with Judaism. [7] Transfer of membership
is relatively uncommon; probably no more than 5 percent
of adults have shifted from the religious group of their
birth to another of the three major religious groups. [8] Even
membership in small, private associations is substantially,
although by no means completely, along religious lines.
It is on the basis of such facts that Kennedy, Herberg,
and others have suggested that America has, not a single,
but a triple melting pot: We are witnessing the gradual
amalgamation of groups within the three major religious
traditions but little assimilation among them. Although

the ethnic lines which formerly coincided with and reenforced religious divisions may gradually be fading, the religious lines of distinction remain clear.

Is this indeed the case? We explored some aspects of the question in Chapter Three. By reexamining it here we can find some of the general principles involved in group identification and withdrawal and can apply them to the issue of assimilation. It is clear that religious divisions, with some reinforcing ethnic aspects, maintain a great deal of vitality in contemporary America. Are the lines of division as sharp as they appear, or do they hide a deeper tendency toward assimilation to common patterns? What factors give salience to an ethnic religion as a reference group in contrast to other possible reference groups? The answers to these questions must be sought on two levels. To some degree, the members of ethnic-religious groups are responding to the same forces that affect members of all other religious groups. What requires explanation is not the particular elements of ethnic religion, but the trends among all religions. In some measure, however, ethnic-religious groups are responding to forces that affect them uniquely or particularly strongly.

It is well to recognize first that ethnic religions are sharing in the "return to religion" that has affected the whole society. Although there is wide disagreement on the intrinsic value of contemporary religious developments, there is extensive agreement on an explanation for them: Having overplayed the power of science, having rested too much hope in secular political developments, men are returning to the religious road to salvation. The great personal confusion, anxiety, and suffering of our time encourage this trend.

Before we accept this explanation we need to determine to what men are returning. Is it a return at all? Are the churches of the country, including the ethnic churches, gaining strength as religious organizations, or are they, at least in part, serving simply as a convenient rallying point for secular interests? The argument for "secularization" seems particularly strong with reference to ethnic churches, because the process of adjustment to the dominant society produces extensive change in them. To some interpreters, the process of change in the direction of accommodation to society is, by definition, secularization.

Insofar as this thesis is accepted, the continuing existence of ethnic churches is not a sign of their strength, but of their "weakness," in the sense that they have become more like the churches of the majority and are less vital in the lives of their members. The national creed, the occupational group, and other associations have taken on many of the functions formerly residing in the religious group.

Although there is strong evidence supporting this argument, it certainly does not fully explain current trends. Religion in one sense is the effort to build a defense against man's ultimate problems, to help him bear the most difficult strains of life. The continuing vitality of ethnic-religious groups in the United States is partly to be accounted for by the sharp challenge brought to all religious interpretations of life in the modern world: the depersonalization of life, the crushing of the individual by the processes of technology, the terror of the "lonely crowd"—these are problems that many people have felt very deeply. Every religion affirms the ultimate dignity and importance of the believer, whatever his status. This affirmation is of special importance to a member of a minority group. Whatever other means he may use to protest discrimination against him and to struggle with his many problems, he is likely to turn to religion. The nature of his religious expression will vary greatly, depending upon his total situation; but throughout all the expressions one finds the affirmation of the dignity of the individual, whatever discriminations and affronts he may meet in the world.

One of the central themes of contemporary sociology is the description and analysis of the sense of insignificance, the rootlessness, the alienation, of many persons in modern society. The increased specialization of interests, the mobility, the bringing together into interdependent communities of individuals with widely different backgrounds, all make it difficult to establish relaxed and informal contacts, to have a sense of some vital connection. There is evidence that this phenomenon helps to explain some aspects of prejudice (I belong, says the prejudiced person), of some of the more exuberant varieties of patriotism (I am strong, says the chauvinist), and of some aspects of religion (I have a home, says the believer).[9]

We have emphasized that continued affiliation with an ethnic-religious group is, to an important degree, simply one aspect of the larger picture of religious identity today. Yet there are many ways in which ethnic-religious groups are dealing with special problems and circumstances. Our interpretation would be very inadequate if these were disregarded. From the point of view of the sociology of religion we would expect Judaism in America, for example, to be sharply modified as it develops within the structure of a system different in so many ways from the Eastern European societies of the nineteenth century—the ancestral background of well over half of American Jews. Continued identification with Judaism is possible, for many people, only if it does not conflict with new identifications with nation, with occupational group, and other reference groups that have become important to them. Thus there is change and there is continuity; there is continued identification with Judaism, but it is identification with a religion that is progressively more similar to those around it and more congruent with its setting and the nonreligious inclinations of its adherents. Those for whom specific beliefs and rites have intrinsic merit can only look upon this as deterioration; those who consider beliefs and rites as agencies for the achievement of some conception of the good life are more concerned with the results of the change.

Whatever the value stand taken, one must recognize the pull of opposite forces. "On the one side is the long, self-conscious history of Jews as a distinct people, with a vital religious and cultural tradition; there is the renewed sense of common weal and a common fate brought about by prejudice, by recent persecutions, by the reestablishment of Israel; there is the recency of migration of most Jews to the United States. On the other side is the speed with which many Jews have penetrated to the middle and upper strata of American society, thus giving them a strong sense of identity with that society; there is freedom of religion, public education, and the relative absence of barriers to economic and political activity; there is the increase in congregational church polity, with strong influence from the laymen; there are the different national origins that erect some barriers to a sense of common Jewishness. Under the influence of these various forces, Judaism has changed, yet it has retained its clear identity." [10]

When studied in the social setting, the continued or even revitalized emphasis of ethnic-religious groups on doctrinal distinctiveness is not surprising. After the language battle is lost and other cultural differences obscured, emphasis on doctrinal differences may increase because they have a heavier load to carry. Even the influence of the family is ambivalent, although probably more largely on the side of continuity. The cultural value placed on family solidarity; the appeal not to disgrace or to isolate the parents; the pride in transmittal of a vigorous cultural tradition; the choice of playmates and group associations; the barriers to intermarriage (very closely related, functionally, to the preservation of the group)—all these and other influences of the family certainly reinforce continuing identification with the ethnic group. Yet the family cannot escape the impact of its surroundings. Patterns that develop in one society create strains in another; and the family, as the carrier of many of these strains, promotes change in many unintended ways.

It is widely assumed that in a period of rapid change, the family is a conservative agency. Parents try to train their children as they were trained; they resist the forces of the new environment that are pulling the children into unaccustomed ways. The reference groups of the two generations are different, giving them different standards of judgment to some degree, with resulting conflict. In a rapidly changing situation, parents often become confused; they develop "disturbed and inconsistent images of their children's future," as Margaret Mead puts it.[11] Were this the whole picture, the family would be a source of enormous strain. But does it not also serve as a bridge, preparing the way for change? Alex Inkeles has found that parents among Russian emigrés did not simply transmit the old, because that was what was in them; they also saw the changes around them and actively shaped their children to deal with the new situation.[12] Further study of the conditions that promote the various tendencies in family influence is needed.

Opposition to intermarriage is another way in which family influence is widely assumed to promote ethnic-religious group continuation. As we noted in Chapter Three the data substantially support this thesis, and yet not so clearly, it appeared, as is generally believed. The rates of religious intermarriage, in fact, vary widely, alerting us to the need for exploring the conditions under which intermarriage occurs frequently or rarely. Many studies indicate that intermarriage is at a minimum when religious difference is reinforced by national, class, language, residential, and other differences. When these supporting differences disappear, intermarriage increases. Moreover, intermarriage is probably cumulative: children of mixed marriages are more likely to marry outside the group than are children of endogamous unions.

Almost all research in this area gives *general* data concerning intermarriage rates. Overall percentages obscure internal differences. We would be better served by careful attention to the variables associated with religious group endogamy and those associated with exogamy, whatever the present empirical distribution. We could then say: insofar as these conditions prevail, intermarriage rates are likely to be at a given level. The long-run trends seem to me to be strengthening most of the conditions which increase intermarriage—the decrease of religious differences, the reduction of supporting lines of differentiation, the cumulative effect of past mixed marriages. These trends are not strong; family and ethnic-religious groups are still closely associated; but the "triple melting pot" thesis needs to be held somewhat lightly.

Prejudice and discrimination are additional important factors influencing the degree of identification with an ethnic group and its religious heritage. Their effects are ambivalent: when they are strong, there are pressures to escape the group, tendencies toward self-hatred, and intragroup conflict. Yet there are also pressures toward group identity and solidarity, pride and loyalty to the group, emphasis on its past greatness and its present achievements, the development of organizations to oppose discrimination.

Prejudice may lead one to declare with Theodor Herzl: "We are a people—the enemy makes us a people." In general, it appears that pressure against a strong group makes it stronger; it increases the morale of its members and heightens their sense of identity. Pressure against a weak group demoralizes the members, heightens intragroup conflict, accentuates the tendencies toward self-hatred and programs of escape (most of them symbolic).

When prejudice and discrimination are on the decline, it is easier to be a group member; there is less punishment, less loss of self-esteem; but fewer forces of defensive solidarity are set in motion. The weaker the group, the more the identification of its members is increased by a situation in which prejudice and discrimination are being reduced. A strong group may find it more difficult to maintain its separate identity under such favorable circumstances. If this proposition is correct—and I state it only as a tentative hypothesis—one would expect the American Negro group to gain in solidarity, in strength, in pride, in the readiness of its members to identify with it—as prejudice and discrimination are reduced; for Negroes have been weak, in the sense of a lack of economic, political, and educational weapons. Identity with Judaism, on the other hand, may be made less likely when there is little prejudice and discrimination. Other reference groups gain in importance when the overwhelming needs for protection and for fulfillment rest less heavily on the ethnic community.

The functions of identification with an ethnic-religious group can be studied, not only by analysis of the group as a whole, but by the examination of internal differentiation. Variations in belief, in organizational structure, in religious aesthetics, and other aspects of religious life are closely related to differences in secular status and experience. The proliferation of separate churches and sects can best be explained, not by disagreements over dogma and rite, but by variation in needs, values, and experiences in a heterogeneous society. As Richard Niebuhr has shown,[13] different classes, races, ethnic groups, and regions develop different religious values and structures. Although Niebuhr referred primarily to variation among Protestant groups, the basic thesis can be applied to Catholicism and Judaism as well. Denominations, to be sure, do not appear within the structure of Catholicism, but the great diversity of the membership of the Catholic Church is reflected in the wide range of its activities and styles of communication. The Catholic Church is in one sense not unlike an American political party, spanning the range from Senator Goldwater to Senator Case, or from Senator Eastland to Senator Humphrey. Those who picture it as a monolithic structure, homogeneous in outlook and uniform in influence, fail to recognize the degree to which religion is affected by culture, class, occupation, educational level, and other secular facts. Such a book as Paul Blanshard's *American Freedom and Catholic Power* [14] pays too little attention to changes through time. (His data range over a fifty-year period with little distinction being drawn among various periods.) It pays too little attention to the distinction between official declaration and the actions of laymen (a distinction that appears clearly, for example, in the relative inability of Puerto Rican bishops to influence the 1960 election for governor of Puerto Rico).

It would, of course, be an error to overlook the forces supporting the continuing distinctiveness of Catholicism. It is scarcely surprising that a church whose historical roots are in ancient and medieval Europe should be different in many ways from, let us say, Congregationalism, with its roots in early modern England and America. When other forces are added—such as the relative recency of immigration of a large part of America's Catholic population, the international structure of the Church, the relatively greater regional, class, and occupational homogeneity of the membership, compared with Protestantism—one recognizes that there are forces that help to preserve a distinctive Catholic tradition and close identification with it on the part of most members.

Some of these forces, however, are less powerful than they have been, and the Catholic Church, like all other religious groups, is being strongly influenced by the contemporary situation. When a minority group becomes more highly differentiated internally, with different degrees of mobility and of contact with other groups, with widely different associations with the economic, political, and educational structures of the total society, religious differentiation inevitably appears. The reference groups with which a professional person feels identified are to some degree different from those of an artisan or merchant; the kinds of personal tensions with which religion attempts to deal are different for members of the middle and upper classes than for members of the lower class; protection against *anomie* (normlessness) doubtless requires, not some vague attachment to a heterogeneous group, but a close institutional attachment to a group whose total life-style corresponds to one's needs and inclinations. It requires a feeling of direct participation with one's peers, with a group in which one feels entirely at home. Human beings who are not quite certain where they belong—there has been so much change and mobility—want very much to assert unambiguously: "I belong; here, at least, there is no doubt, I belong. To the nation, yes; to the lodge; to my occupational group; but if there is any doubt about these, above all I belong to my religious group, about which no one will raise a doubt." Thus the association with a subdivision of an ethnic-religious group is an attempt to deal with the same problems that identity with the larger group represents.

The American environment helps to preserve distinctive religious groups even in the face of powerful tendencies toward assimilation. This results from the fact that both the ideology of the nation and social and geographical mobility discourage many aspects of ethnic-group survival, but they permit religious differentiation. Those who would like to see a continuation of ethnic identity and traditional variation, therefore, are led to emphasize their strictly religious meaning. In his account of "the uprooted," Handlin observed this tendency: "Struggling against heavy odds to save something of the old ways, the immigrants directed into their faith the whole weight of their longing to be connected with the past." [15] Their children and grandchildren follow this pattern, although not without differences of meaning.[16]

It thus appears that in this generation, at least, the lines among Catholic, Protestant, and Jew remain clear, despite the reduction in secular differences among the constituent groups. To some degree, however, this is true because close identity with a religious group does not alienate one from the total society. Religion has become somewhat marginal —a brand name—while basic allegiance is given to "the American Way of Life." [17] Religious difference is freely permitted, hence it becomes the legatee of all the ethnic differences that might otherwise have continued more strongly. To be a Catholic or a Jew is much less to be considered alien than even a generation ago. (The testimony of the 1960 presidential election, although somewhat ambiguous in this regard, largely supports this view.) Thus the dysfunction of religious-group identity is reduced while its functions continue. If this argument is valid, the continuing vitality of Catholicism and Judaism is not a sign of the slowing down of the "Americanization" of Catholics and Jews. It is, indeed, a sign of how deeply involved they are in the total pattern of American society.[18]

What can we expect in the years ahead from the processes of group identification and withdrawal? First, there is the inevitability of continuing change in the doctrines, rites, and group structure of religious organizations. In analyses of this question one sometimes gets the impression that the third generation has arrived at some point of equilibrium, that, although there was clearly a sharp change between the first and second and between the second and third generations, a point of relative stability has now been reached. One might more readily expect a continuing "Americanization," a continuing adjustment to the setting in which religious groups are found. This probably will not mean much loss of membership, for although the distinctiveness of belonging will be reduced, so also will some of the penalties associated with identification with a minority group. Professional staffs will sustain the group by emphasizing its uniqueness while participating in a process which reduces that uniqueness. This is in no way to suggest hypocrisy on their part, but to indicate the way in which the total field of influences within which they work inevitably affects their responses. For the layman, continuing identification with his religious group will not necessarily represent the strength of the religious tradition. The tradition will undergo continuing modification, partly as a result of his influence. But in a vast and complicated society, in a day of depersonalization, the religious group will help one to answer the difficult question, Who Am I? At the same time, occupational, political, and other reference groups that cut across religious lines will continue to reduce the sense of the religious group as a total community. Future developments of ethnic-religious groups depend in part, of course, on the external situation in which the members find themselves. Barring a sharp increase in discrimination, we are likely to continue to see the paradox of continued identification accompanied by a deeper and deeper involvement in the other groups of our society.

II. Contemporary Pluralism or Historical Pluralism

It remains to ask, what are the consequences for the total society of continued identification—to the degree and in the manner that we have suggested—with separate ethnic-religious groups? This leads us into one of the central questions of contemporary sociology: How does a complex, urban society manage to exist as a healthy system; how does it establish and maintain a sufficient level of integration and consensus to maintain order and carry through the necessary accommodations among its heterogeneous peoples? It cannot rely on what Durkheim called the "mechanical solidarity" of a relatively undifferentiated community; and a free society resists an integration that is imposed by coercion. Does it not, therefore, at the least require consensus on its fundamental values, on religion, which is often thought to be the source of integration at the deepest level? Can it afford to be indifferent to the continued vitality of ethnic-religious groups which divide a society in important ways?

It might be said parenthetically that modern societies had only begun (that is, within the last few generations) to struggle with this question when it abruptly became a problem for the entire world. Before Marconi, the Wright Brothers, and Einstein we might, perhaps, have been entitled simply to ask: How can the diverse members of a modern society live together in trust and cooperation? Is similarity necessary? Is tolerance enough? But now, having only begun to develop patterns that deal with the question on the societal level, we discover it to be a world problem. The question of affiliation or rejection of an ethnic group on the national level seems almost trivial, because the differences among groups are small, compared with the massive difficulties associated with group identification in a world made suddenly small. The question is not trivial, however, because only after we have understood and developed patterns appropriate to the needs of modern societies can we hope to create a system for the world in which similarities are not coerced and differences do not divide.

On this question we are confronted again by a paradox: the integration of a complex and heterogeneous society requires both basic commonalities and freedom to be different. These are readily granted as important values of American society: but they are not always recognized as functionally necessary patterns for a heterogeneous, changing society. There are, of course, a great many common elements in Protestantism, Catholicism, and Judaism—elements that have been increased in the last several decades. The classicist in each tradition insists that the reduction of distinctiveness is a loss, and from his point of view it is. His point of view, however, is unlikely to prevail. The reduction, particularly, of the parochial, the exclusive, the claims of absolute truth seems inevitable in our kind of society. It is dysfunctional in a mobile and diverse society to have a group of religions, each of which claims some kind of ultimate superiority; the elements of Protestantism, Catholicism, and Judaism which sponsor such claims are disruptive. Claims by Protestants that the Bible is the final and literal truth, by Catholics that theirs is the only true church, by Jews that they are the chosen people can only exacerbate the divisions of a society. (The believer will say, "But these are the truth." Such a view is never disproved; but it may become a meaningless claim to another generation.)

In a diverse society in which absolute religious claims are asserted, three things may happen: the society will be split seriously; or the differences will be reduced; or the traditional religious assertions will lose force, while a new unifying system of beliefs and actions will be developed, often around national and patriotic themes. All three of these things are happening in the United States, the last being perhaps the strongest tendency. "The American Way of Life" becomes the operative faith to a substantial degree. Those who wish to relate the national faith to one of the traditional religions are free to do so, provided they do not challenge any of the basic premises of Americanism. Emphasis on religious variation thus tends to shift the burden of integration to other parts of the social system—particularly to the sentiments of nationalism. If this interpretation is correct, universalistic religions may face self-defeating limits to the insistence upon their differences.

The other side of the paradox also requires examination. On the contemporary scene, in fact, the need for a common core of values is doubtless more readily granted than the need for diversity. The latter, therefore, requires special emphasis. The integration of any society, however homogeneous it may seem to an outsider, is pluralistic; it requires the harmonizing of different individual roles and different groups. The vast complexity of a modern society extends pluralism to an extraordinary degree. The constant interaction of people with different national and religious backgrounds, with different occupations and different levels of education, makes mutual tolerance, as the minimum

degree of accommodation, a vital necessity. (That pluralism is the only imaginable pattern for a peaceful world
need scarcely be mentioned.) A century ago, John Stuart
Mill observed that a diversity of religious views was essential to a free, heterogeneous society, to minimize any
authoritarian tendencies in the church and to maximize
the autonomy of religious influences from other centers of
power. Contemporary political sociology, drawing on a
long tradition, has documented the importance of a strong
network of private associations, standing between the individual and the state, if democracy is to thrive.[19] A vigorous
group of partially competing religious organizations may
be among the most significant of such associations. Their
importance to the members lends them strength to coun-
ter the opposite dangers of lack of meaningful attachments
in a changing world on one hand and the threat of domination by the state on the other. The fact that our major
religious divisions cut across such other lines as class, occupation, and race, helps greatly to prevent the cumulative
reinforcement of dividing forces that can split a society
into warring segments.[20]

The point of view just expressed is, I believe, widely
supported. Yet it leaves problems unexplored that deserve
our attention. I would like to conclude Part I, therefore,
by raising some questions that are usually kept muted. Is
the continuing separation of American religious subcommunities—to the degree that this exists—a good thing?
Is pluralism the best arrangement for a complex society?
Are signs of the weakening of the internal cohesion of the
traditional groups, intermarriage particularly, unhappy indicators of a loss of strength and fervor? These are, of
course, value questions; and in the paragraphs that follow,
I will take a frankly evaluative position.

For the most part, those who take a liberal view of
American society support religious pluralism. Distinctive
religious traditions, all free to develop in their own ways,
are essential to the religious quest and to a democratic

society. To the individual they represent freedom and yet a significant tie to his own heritage. To the society they represent the kind of competing points of view that help to maintain flexibility, because there is no official religion to give undue sanctity to our imperfect human institutions. The liberal view would only add, as we have noted, that the separate religious groups should not be thoroughly separate communities, distinctive in occupation, class, region, and ethnic origin, as well as religion, because such piling up of differences leads to serious conflict. It is best when the members of each religious group are dispersed through the geographical, class, and occupational systems.

There is some conservative challenge to this view. Some Catholics believe that a genuinely healthy society and full individual salvation are possible only when all men have returned to the one true church. Most Catholics who take this view have learned patience in the American scene, indicating a kind of qualified acceptance of pluralism. Some Protestants look upon Catholics and Jews as at least slightly un-American and wonder why they are so recalcitrant in becoming Methodists or Baptists or Presbyterians.

Now I am much closer to the liberal than to the conservative view. I am not, however, entirely happy with pluralism as it is usually described and would like to comment on some of its possible dysfunctions. In a period of such dramatic change as man is now experiencing, the need for new ideas and new actions—including religious ideas and actions—is enormous. Most of us are religiously lazy. We take part in the search for new political forms, new economic ideas, new ways to build our cities, new technological processes, but our conceptions of religion are static. This distinction should not be drawn too sharply, of course. One need only mention the continuing use of the ideas of Thomas Jefferson and Adam Smith to indicate how difficult it is to sort out the universal from the local and temporary in government and economics as well as in religion. These giants are complex mixtures of the contemporary and the outmoded in economic and political affairs. The tendency to use them as fully adequate guides today demonstrates that it is not only religion that needs to be "demythologized," to use the current term.

But our concern here is with religion, and I think one can argue that emphasis on distinctive pluralistic traditions implies a measure of religious stagnation and isolation. The best way to justify continued separation is to point to different origins, histories, and traditions. To some degree, American religious groups are like our Indian tribes: they lose their liberals to the "secular" world, because the emphasis on preservation of distinctiveness is inherently backward-looking. The churches "boom" in this day of upsetting change and continual crisis; but the messages they preach are tuned to an earlier time, so the people are "secularized"—indifferent and unbelieving and religiously ill informed—even while they participate in the "boom."

Viewing this situation, I certainly would not want to take an antipluralist position, to argue in favor of some one religious orthodoxy. A unified church would all the more surely be conservative and static; and in view of the great heterogeneity of people in a large society, no one religious view is able to reach all the people.

Is there any way out of this dilemma? I would like to suggest a possible road by introducing the concept of "contemporary pluralism," in contrast to the more familiar "historical pluralism." The latter might be briefly defined in these terms: Preservation of ties to the religious community (and ethnic group—for some of the same questions arise in this area) of one's parents is good; respect its traditions; a free society must encourage this in the name of tolerance, flexibility, and individual freedom. I would argue that there is more than a little nostalgia and sentimentality connected with this idea. These qualities are often heightened by those professionally identified with a group, whose preservation as a distinctive entity is necessary for their professional existence. They are also heightened by persons working in the field of intergroup relations and other liberally minded individuals who, again with generous motives, support and encourage group-identity as a way of developing mutual respect and tolerance.

Historical pluralism may be crucial and valuable in one period and not in another. At a time when the development of pride and self-confidence and feelings of identity to something smaller than the baffling, complex, total society are important, historical pluralism may contribute to religious growth and a strong relationship between religion and society. But to continue to promote religious and ethnic separation in a new context, when the tie to the earlier situation has been broken, may be unwise. Perhaps the necessary pluralism today is not a process whereby each of us binds his children to the ancestral religious groups, while teaching them to respect the rights of others who are different. Perhaps we need to open up interaction and choice among several contemporary efforts to struggle with the human condition, each a hybrid, each a product of religious contact and growth.

This point is made somewhat more easily with respect to ethnic groups and perhaps I can clarify my argument by a brief reference to this related question. In Hawaii, for example, many people say: Won't it be a shame when there are no longer distinctive Chinese, Japanese, native Hawaiian, and other communities and subcultures. (They are, indeed, being preserved in less and less complete ways, religiously and otherwise.) For myself I doubt that the decline of distinctive subcommunities is unfortunate. A dynamic view of life and society sees this decline as inevitable. Contemporary life cannot be carried on by the preservation of styles, however dignified and intrinsically important in their points of origin, in vastly different contexts. What would be unfortunate would be the loss of contributions from each of the now declining communities to the new heterogeneous and varied culture of modern society. Choice and variety for the individual and flexibility for our systems of belief and action are perhaps a higher ideal than choice and variety among traditional groups.

We cannot cling to the culturally and religiously integrated patterns of the past. If we think we are doing so, we hide the loss of their vitality and the emergence of competing systems of value (nationalism as a religion, for example). The inherent rigidity of historical pluralism obscures the new problems faced by men today, for which we need vital contemporary religious thought and action.

This difficulty is increased by the very success of American society. There is less pressure on privileged people to revise their received religions than on the underprivileged. They are more likely to support a religious revival than a reformation. This means that if great new issues arise, as a result of dramatic changes in the life of man, the churches of the privileged are not well equipped to deal with them. Subterranean religious movements develop; quasi religions appear. Perhaps careful study of this fact can help, in some small measure, to make it less probable.

FOOTNOTES

1. For recent statements see Erich Rosenthal, "Acculturation Without Assimilation?" *American Journal of Sociology*, Nov., 1960, pp. 275-288; Amitai Etzioni, "The Ghetto—a Re-evaluation," *Social Forces*, March, 1959, pp. 255-262.
2. See Robert Bierstedt, *The Social Order*, New York: McGraw-Hill, 1957, chap. 8.
3. Shibutani, Tamotsu. "Reference Groups as Perspectives," *American Journal of Sociology*, May, 1955, pp. 562-569; Robert Merton, *Social Theory and Social Structure*, rev. ed., The Free Press, 1957, chapter 9.
4. According to the 1940 Census, nearly one-fifth of the white population spoke a mother tongue other than English. Although later reports from the Census do not give us such data, it is doubtless true that the proportion has dropped,

along with the proportion of the foreign-born. The decline will not be abrupt, however. Over 60 percent of the foreign-speaking group in 1940 were native-born. See Lowry Nelson, "Speaking of Tongues," *American Journal of Sociology*, Nov., 1948, pp. 202-210.

5. *The Population of the United States*, The Free Press, 1959, p. 771.

6. Munch, Peter. "Social Adjustments Among Wisconsin Norwegians," *American Sociological Review*, Dec., 1949, vol. 14, pp. 780-787.

7. See the U.S. Bureau of the Census, "Religion Reported by the Civilian Population of the United States: March, 1957," *Current Population Reports*, Series P-20, No. 79; *Public Opinion News Service* (the Gallup Poll), 20 March 1955; and the *Catholic Digest*, Jan., 1953.

8. The Gallup Poll gives a figure of 4 percent (see *Public Opinion News Service*, 20 March 1955). Gerhard Lenski, using data from a random sample of the Detroit area, 1958, indicates that 93 percent of Catholics and 95 percent of Protestants remain in the groups within which they were raised. (See Gerhard Lenski, *The Religious Factor*, Doubleday & Company, Inc., 1961.)

9. At this point a vital question of values arises. The supporter of religion will say, Surely it is better that men search for an anchorage in religion than in prejudice or chauvinism. The critic of religion is likely to respond, There is some evidence that the more religious are also the more prejudiced, and that piety arms patriotism with an excessively good conscience —these are not functional alternatives. Clearly, some kinds of religious inclination are associated with bigotry and chauvinism; others are an antidote to these faults. A basic challenge to the scientist and the religionist is to describe the differences and discover the conditions that promote either relation.

10. Yinger, J. Milton. *Religion, Society and the Individual*. The Macmillan Company, 1957, p. 288.

11. Haring, Douglas, ed. *Personal Character and Cultural Milieu*. Syracuse University Press, 1949, p. 560.

12. Inkeles, Alex. "Social Change and Social Character: The Role of Parental Mediation," *Journal of Social Issues*, 1955, 11: 12-23.

13. *The Social Sources of Denominationalism*. New York: Henry Holt & Co., Inc., 1929; reprinted, Hamden, Conn.: The Shoestring Press, 1954.

14. The Beacon Press, rev. ed., 1958.

15. Handlin, Oscar. *The Uprooted*. Little, Brown & Co., 1951, p. 117.

16. See Nathan Glazer, "The Jewish Revival in America," *Commentary*, Dec., 1955, pp. 493-499; and Jan., 1956, pp. 17-24.

17. This thesis is developed in Will Herberg, *Protestant—Catholic—Jew*, Doubleday & Company, Inc., 1955.

18. See Herbert J. Gans, "American Jewry; Present and Future," *Commentary*, May, 1956, pp. 422-430; and "The Future of American Jewry," *Commentary*, June, 1956, pp. 555-563.

19. For a cogent statement of this thesis, see William Kornhauser, *The Politics of Mass Society*, The Free Press, 1959.

20. Although we are primarily concerned in this chapter with the social forces involved in identification or withdrawal from religious groups, particularly those with some ethnic aspects, we note in passing that the general principles involved apply to racial groups as well. When the race line converges with other lines of division—when persons of different races tend also to be of a different class, occupation, religion, income, education, residence, subcultural style of life, and historical experience—the sharpness of the racial line is at a maximum. When these other differentia fall away, however, acculturation, desegregation, and finally integration begin.

II.

The Sources and Research Tasks
of the Sociology of Religion

IT IS often valuable, in the study of a science, to investigate its origins and to examine its relationship to bordering sciences. The problems that become central and the assumptions and perspectives that influence their study are affected by origins and by the work of related disciplines.

Anthropology and sociology are closely connected—indeed indistinguishable—at many points. This is nowhere more nearly true than in the study of religion. The examination of some aspects of their relationship in Chapter Five can serve as an illustration of the ways in which the sociology of religion has been influenced by other approaches to religion. A full commentary would also explore the relationships to history, biblical studies, philosophy, theology, and psychology, to mention perhaps the most important fields of study with respect to this question.

Chapter Six outlines the major research areas of the sociology of religion and Chapter Seven illustrates the application of a concept drawn from general sociology to religious phenomena. This discussion may serve to show the extent to which the full range of sociological theory and method is required in the analysis of religion.

5

The Influence of Anthropology
on Sociological Theories
of Religion

IN EXPLORING this topic, we are met at the very outset with problems of definition and distinction. It it unnecessary here to discuss the many definitions of anthropology and the different conceptions of its appropriate range of interests. I believe that it would be generally agreed, however, that insofar as anthropology is concerned with the study of such topics as religion, it approaches the area where it is closest to sociology. The question is: How close is that? In principle, the two disciplines are almost identical to the degree that they involve efforts to develop analytic and systematic theories of religion. There may well be differences in method and in the type of data given primary attention, but it is difficult to conceive of a theoretical "anthropology of religion" separate from "sociology of religion."

If this point of view is accepted, we can distinguish only roughly between anthropological and sociological studies of religion. Some separation can be made on the basis of the professional identity of the workers in the area, on the degree of emphasis to primitive or modern societies, on the extent to which cultural or social interactional aspects of religion are given primary attention. But even these criteria permit us to develop only a thin line of distinction. It is not always clear who is to be classified as an anthropologist: Tylor certainly, but Malinowski not quite so certainly, and Radcliffe-Brown less certainly still. Nor is attention to primitive societies a sure sign of the anthropological approach of a study, as the work of Durkheim and Mauss, and more recently Goode and Swanson, demonstrates. A distinction based on the degree of attention to culture or social interaction is even less clear. Professor Kroeber believed that sociology was concerned with churches, for example, primarily "as operating systems of interacting people," while anthropology was concerned *also* (n.b.) with their cultures. I find it difficult to see how the sociologist can profitably study "the relations of the communicants" independent of the beliefs and other cultural items they share in common. What Kroeber required of the anthropologist, that he study social and cultural facts together, is equally incumbent on the sociologist, although there may be some difference in emphasis.

By this introduction I have almost demolished the topic of this chapter—almost, but not quite. One can certainly draw some distinction between the work of Malinowski and Durkheim, or between the approach to religion of Howells and Parsons. It is my conviction, however, that in an advanced science of religion such distinctions must be lost. This conviction is reflected in the following formal definition of the sociology of religion. It is "the scientific study of the ways in which society, culture, and personality . . . influence religion—influence its origin, its doctrines, its practices, the types of groups which express it, the kinds of leadership, etc. And, oppositely, it is the study of the ways in which religion affects society, culture, and personality—the processes of social conservation and social change, the structure of normative systems, the satisfaction or frustration of personality needs, etc." [1]

In commenting on the influence of anthropology on the development of such a discipline, I am not primarily concerned with tracing direct descent of ideas from individual *A* to individual *B*, as if I were dealing with a problem of diffusion or acculturation—or perhaps of archaeology. We shall rather be interested in a broad sketch of the ways in which anthropological data, methods, and theories have affected sociological studies of religion.

I. The Influence of Evolutionary Theory

The evolutionary conceptions of Tylor, Frazer, and others were widely cited by sociologists and formed the basis of their descriptions of religious institutions. It is indicative of the lack of a genuinely sociological view of religion that Spencer, Sumner, Giddings, and many others, could have used classic evolutionism, despite its thoroughly individualistic and rationalistic approach, without any major criticisms. It should be stressed that the evolutionary view was not incorporated into a sociological theory of religion. It was simply taken over and accepted by many persons called sociologists. One can only speculate on the consequences of this strong reliance of early sociologists on anthropological data and theories. It may actually have slowed the development of a sociology of religion by reducing interest in the study of religion among students of contemporary societies. If one looks at religion through the eyes of Tylor, Frazer, Spencer, and Giddings, he is not likely to conceive of it as an important part of the life of modern man. Evolutionary theory may also have led sociologists to raise relatively less fruitful questions about religion— what was its origin, is it cognitively true—than did other approaches to religion. On the other hand, early anthropology was vital in establishing the necessary comparative view and in overcoming the cultural myopia that prevents an objective analysis of religion.

When we turn to the writers who are generally regarded as the founders of modern sociology, particularly to Weber and Durkheim, we find that their interest in religion is not limited to the descriptive level and to borrowed theory.[2] In the case of Weber, there is litle direct influence from anthropological work. His studies of religion draw widely on history, classics, economics, philosophy, Marxism, and anti-Marxism. But neither his data nor his theoretical perspectives are drawn from anthropology to any significant degree. This is perhaps partly attributable to the fact that the vital center of his work—the study of the origin, types, and structure of capitalism and of complex societies generally—demanded research in other directions. Those who followed the Weber lead—and they make up probably the largest group of writers in the sociology of religion—show little influence from anthropology: These include his colleague Troeltsch, Tawney, Richard Neibuhr, E. T. Clark, Wellman Warner, and many others. Perhaps it should be noted, parenthetically, that in his attention to the time dimension, Weber shares a concern with cultural anthropology that is greatly curtailed in extreme functionalism. This attention to background sources (if not to ultimate origins) leads in his work to some of the strengths and weaknesses for a sociology of religion that the same attention produces in anthropology. It sometimes obscures the contemporary meaning of a religious belief or practice; yet lack of knowledge of the past surely leads to errors of interpretation.

With Durkheim, of course, the situation is different. In many ways his major study of religion is a technical monograph on totemism in Australia. But Durkheim was first and last a theorist, and he used the data, drawn from the work of several anthropologists, primarily to construct a thoroughgoing sociologistic theory of religion. By sociologistic I mean a theory that so heavily emphasizes the importance of the fact of society as the starting point of religion that it obscures other significant factors. Durkheim seems to accept the attempt to find the origin of religion as a central task. In his characteristic polemic style, he attacks as inadequate the existing theories of origin, especially those of Tylor, Spencer, and Müller. By the time he has finished, however, it is clear that he is working out, not a theory of religious origins, but an analysis of the continuing place of religion in social life. His work bears the mark of Comte and of Robertson Smith, basically a historian, more than of anthropology.

II. The Influence of Functional Theory

With the development of functional theory the influence of anthropology on the sociology of religion becomes more direct and important. Functionalism is not solely a product of anthropology, of course; it is one of those basic scientific orientations that appear in widely different fields "when the time is ripe." Indeed, a sociological functionalism can be traced from Comte and Spencer to Durkheim, Schäffle, Small, Cooley, and on down to the present scene. The use of a functional approach by anthropologists in the interpretation of religion and magic, however, has been a particularly important influence on the sociology of religion during the past thirty years.[3] Functionalism has been primary among the influences that have brought into the sociology of religion the idea that religion is part of a complex social system, not simply an irrational survival. The concept that religion is functionally connected with the very fact of society, that it is necessary for its survival and the maintenance of equilibrium in human affairs, required a thorough reexamination of the picture drawn by earlier sociologists. This point of view is more readily achieved in the study of the less highly compartmentalized primitive societies than in the analysis of differentiated societies.

There are difficulties and dangers, however, in the transfer of functional analysis from primitive to complex societies. The difficulties derive primarily from the sharper separation of institutions in modern life and from disagreement over the definition of religion. In my judgment, a great deal of religion today is given other names—nationalism, communism, or even science (as a way of life, not as a method). Such a remark clearly implies a very broad definition of religion, but a definition that may be more fruitful than a narrow one in helping us understand human behavior in the contemporary world.

The difficulties that sociologists face in drawing upon a functional analysis developed by anthropologists are matched by the dangers. These derive largely from the failure to make adjustments in the theory when applying it to rapidly changing and heterogeneous societies. I need only mention Merton's well known criticisms of extreme functional theory to suggest some of the problems involved in its application to complex societies. He discusses three postulates that he believes are not necessary to functional analysis, that in fact transform it from a theory to an ideology, but which are frequently found: The postulate of the functional unity of a society—that every standardized activity or belief is functional, that is, necessary and useful for the whole social system; the postulate that every social form has a positive function; the postulate of indispensability—that certain functions are necessary to survival of a society and/or that particular cultural or social forms are indispensable in carrying out these functions.[4] Few writers develop the overly simplified version of functionalism that Merton criticizes, but there are some close approximations of it; for example, in Malinowski's well known words:

And here into this play of emotional forces, into this supreme dilemma of life and final death, religion steps in, selecting the positive creed, the comforting view, the culturally valuable belief in immortality, in the spirit independent of the body, and in the continuance of life after death. In the various ceremonies at death, in commemoration and communion with the departed, and worship of ancestral ghosts, religion gives body and form to the saving beliefs.[5]

This assumption of positive functions in Malinowski's statement is matched by many sociologists today. Hertzler writes: "Under the religious impulse, whether theistic or humanistic, men have joy in living; life leads somewhere." [6]

Or, in the words of Kingsley Davis:

Thus the existence of goals beyond this world serves to compensate people for the frustrations they inevitably experience in striving to reach socially acquired and socially valuable ends. It replaces a possibly dangerous aggression with a benevolent faith in the unseen. By giving him a world beyond this one, a sort of invisible shell around the factual sphere, the culture enables the individual to interpret any catastrophe as intermediate and secondary, leaving the road open to ultimate happiness. [7]

Professor Davis is by no means unaware of the qualifications necessary in functional analysis. This awareness is shown particularly in his Introduction to the volume by Goode, 1951. The need is to make this awareness operate in research. One wonders if the consequences of religion are as obvious as they are made to seem in the quotations above. Are they universal; if not, under what conditions do they appear? When there are several religions in one society, is "possibly dangerous aggression" reduced? When a society is divided sharply into classes, does religion serve the same functions as it does in a more homogeneous society? May it not accentuate differences? Fauset writes, in connection with the cults among highly disprivileged urban Negroes, "It must come as a great relief as well as release to such people to enter into the spirit of a group like one of the holiness cults. . . ." [8] It seems to me at least open to doubt whether religion helps disprivileged persons to bear somewhat more gracefully a status which in any event they are powerless to change, or whether it discourages them from seeking out other available responses that might change their status. The results are problematic. We need to seek out the conditions under which various effects are found.

I have not been trying to argue against the functional approach—indeed, I think it is a vital aspect of the sociology of religion. Religion had been seen as anachronistic by many sociologists. Functionalism has helped to refocus interest on religion and relate it to the whole sociocultural complex. One needs to use functionalism with great care, however, with full attention, in Merton's terms, to latent as well as manifest functions and to dysfunctions. We need especially to explore, more than anthropological studies have done, the matter of functional alternatives. Granted the need for *some* sociocultural structure that deals with the ultimate problems of individual and group life, we must explore the range of possible forms that structure may take in a given society.

I can only briefly suggest the extent to which functional theory has come into the sociology of religion. It is found, as we have noted, in Durkheim, and in a somewhat different sense in Weber. The more direct influence of anthropology, however, comes a little later. There are some indications of it in Clifford Kirkpatrick's, *Religion in Human Affairs* (1929), perhaps the first general statement about religion by an American sociologist. The work of Frazer, Tylor, Lang, and Spencer is critically used, and there are many references to Radin, Lowie, Goldenweiser, and Malinowski. Durkheim's theory is discussed; but there are no references to the work of Weber, Troeltsch, and Tawney. The book now seems quite crudely eclectic, yet it indicates the beginnings of a more adequate conceptual scheme.

In a quick survey of ten current introductory sociology texts, I found that five of them draw heavily on anthropological materials for their discussion. The other five make almost no use of anthropology; indeed three of the books make virtually no reference to religion. Four of the texts employ a functional approach; and these are the only ones that move very far beyond description to try to develop a sociology of religion.

The influence of the functional approach is more adequately tested by an examination of recent research papers and systematic studies in the sociology of religion. Perhaps the first thing that strikes one from such an examination is the scarcity of sociological studies of religion. Of approximately five hundred titles that I have used in the preparation of a recent book, scarcely more than thirty are recent (since 1940) sociological studies, if a fairly strict definition is used. If I may be permitted a rough and arbitrary classification, I would place seven of thirty primarily in the Weber tradition. A listing of some of the titles may indicate the focus of interest: "Church-Sect Typology and Socio-Economic Status"; "The Protestant Ethic, Level of Aspiration, and Social Mobility: An Empirical Test"; "From Sect to Church"; "A Comparative Study of the Role of Values in Social Action in Two Southwestern Communities." Four of the papers or books are almost purely descriptive; five involve some current sociological concept that is applied to religious data—role theory, for example. This leaves fourteen studies—systematic statements or monographs—that are strongly affected by the functional approach. If this proportion were to be duplicated in a complete bibliography of recent work in the sociology of religion, it means that about half of the research shows the strong imprint of functionalism and another quarter is to some degree affected by it. It must be said that probably two-thirds of these also show the influence of the Weber approach. Again I must be content with a mere listing of some of the titles to indicate something of the subject matter and the theoretical orientation of these studies: "Why Are the Cults Growing?"; "Some Aspects of Christian Science as Reflected in Letters of Testimony"; "Holiness Religion: Cultural Shock and Social Reorganization"; *Millhands and Preachers*; "Jamaican Revivalist Cults"; *Conservative Judaism: An American Religious Movement*.

Contemporary systematic work in the sociology of religion, although almost all of it has been affected by functionalism, has a broader theoretical base to which we shall refer later. The first book in English under the title

Sociology of Religion, by the late Joachim Wach, drew widely on anthropological studies and developed many valuable sociological concepts, particularly typologies of various kinds, but it did not escape the influence of its basically theological perspective. Systematic work by sociologists is painfully scarce. There are excellent chapters by Williams and Davis (the latter strongly functional) in general texts. Nottingham and Parsons have written brief monographs which draw extensively on anthropological data and concepts; and Professor Parsons discusses religion in almost all of his books, with anthropological materials continually in evidence. His sociology of religion derives most directly from Weber and Durkheim, but the work of Malinowski and other anthropologists is also used.

The most explicit use, in recent years, of the data of primitive societies to develop a sociology of religion is found in William Goode, *Religion Among the Primitives,* and Guy Swanson, *The Birth of the Gods.* The former is limited entirely to an analysis of the ways in which "religion intertwines with other aspects of social life" among five primitive societies. Yet it is strictly a sociology of religion. Its theoretical orientation is drawn from Parsons, Merton, Weber, and Durkheim, and to a lesser degree from the functionalists among anthropologists. Without being too facetious, Goode might have entitled his study, *Les Fonctions Elémentaires de la Vie Religieuse.* He is fully aware of the difficulties involved in transferring his analysis from preliterate to modern societies; but he felt that, in addition to the intrinsic value of a sociology of primitive religions, it might be possible to develop concepts by the study of preliterates that could be tested for wider applicability. In *Birth of the Gods,* Swanson makes use of a wide range of information on religion by selecting fifty representative societies to explore a specific question: Are the beliefs about God and the supernatural world in these societies related in consistent ways to aspects of their social structure? He suggests, to note one of his tentative conclusions, that monotheism occurs most readily in those societies where at least three levels of fairly independent or "sovereign" groups (e.g., family, clan, and tribe) are found, each with distinguishable areas of power.

Sociology of religion in Germany is largely Weberian. In France, Mauss, Halbwachs, and others followed the lead of Durkheim, with extensive use of data from preliterate peoples. More recently, French sociology of religion, particularly the work of LeBras, shows the impact of demography and urban sociology, with little anthropological influence in evidence, although it should be noted that some functionalism appears, as, for example, in the book by Pin, *Pratique Religieuse et Classes Sociales*.

Finally, in this brief reference to the range of studies we should note the appearance of several general statements, either of the sociology of religion or of the sociology of American religion. The first, by the present writer, has as its major theoretical sources Weber, Troeltsch, and Durkheim; but it has also been affected by anthropology from Tylor on, by Lang and Malinowski, by Lowie, Radin, and Howells, and by many other anthropologists. The book by Hoult also draws extensively on anthropological studies. Recent texts by Benson, Moberg, and Vernon show the influence less strongly, but all use anthropological materials and concepts to some degree.[9]

Since I have used a broad definition of the sociology of religion, it may be wise to make a brief reference to Freudian and neo-Freudian theories of religion, in terms of their relationship to anthropology and sociology. We can scarcely give credence to Freud's own version of "the elementary forms of the religious life," to use Durkheim's title. His account of the origins of totemism is an ingenious piece of anthropological reconstruction, utterly beyond testing, which we could see simply as interesting speculation if Freud had not used it as a general theory of the origin of religion. Happily, he moved toward a more adequate functional view, almost in spite of himself: Religion springs from man's helplessness, the demands for justice unfulfilled, the desire to prolong life. These hints of a functional interpretation were elaborated by Jung (who, however, is too individualistic in his analysis to be of much value to a sociology of religion) and especially by Fromm. Fromm is much more aware of the importance of the variation in the sociocultural setting than Freud or Jung. Although his theory is not explicitly functional, it can easily be transposed. In his treatment of Lutheranism, for example, the phrase, "the compulsive quest for certainty . . . is rooted in the need to conquer the unbearable doubt," could be made to read, "the *function* of the compulsive quest . . ." without changing its meaning. Citations in his books make it clear that Fromm has an extensive familiarity with anthropological materials. Although inferences of this sort are hazardous, it seems quite possible that his awareness of cultural and social factors is partly related to this familiarity. The question remains: to what degree have the Freudian and neo-Freudian interpretations of religion—carrying some imprint from anthropology—influenced the sociology of religion. There is very little sign of influence in research papers and monographs. Among those who have worked on systematic theory, however, those who define the sociology of religion in terms that require attention to the personality dimension show the influence of the "culturized" versions of psychoanalytic theory. This is true of the work of Professor Parsons and of the present writer.

III. *Summary*

It may be useful to draw together, in summary, a list of the various converging forces that have created contemporary sociology of religion, and indicate the place of anthropology among them:

1. The Weber-Troeltsch influence (little anthropology).

2. American community studies and ecology (e.g., the work of H. Paul Douglass on city churches and the Lynds' Middletown research). Some of this is occasionally referred to as anthropological in method, but the usage is not clear.

3. The Marxian tradition—and opposition to it. Out of this has come the problem of the relation of religion to other interests and to social change. (Closely related to 1.)

4. The evolutionary school in anthropology. This influence is still to be seen directly in some introductory sociology texts; but it has only a small place in the work of specialists in the sociology of religion.

5. Functionalism. As we have seen, it has been sharply modified, but is vital to the contemporary work.

6. Neo-Freudianism. This appears in the work of those sociologists who have brought personality concepts into their frame of reference.

Perhaps the most prominent aspect of this list is what is left out—most of the work of American cultural anthropologists. Their relative lack of influence on the sociology of religion is certainly not a product of any lack of attention to religion (although in the inventory, *Anthropology Today*, there are very few references to religion). Nor is it a result of an unwillingness on the part of sociologists to use anthropological materials. Sociology has, in fact, courted anthropology rather ardently (with only a few disappointed suitors complaining that it was a useless pursuit). But American anthropology has been quite indifferent to the advances. This is not the place to try to discover why that should be the case. It seems likely, however, that the great influence of the culture-history approach, with its relative lack of attention to theory, its emphasis on the distinctive aspects of each culture, its slowness, therefore, in developing general categories for the observation of data, has been to make the use of its materials difficult for the sociologist of religion. I would not want to suggest that Amercan anthropologists should have handled their material differently. For certain kinds of problems, the culture-history approach is very fruitful. I am only lamenting the fact, as a sociologist of religion, that the dominant emphasis is one that yields less adequate material than a theoretically and sociologically oriented anthropolgy would have produced. American anthropology is complex, of course, with many different emphases within it. For at least twenty-five years it has been possible to be interested in psychology or psychoanalysis and still keep one's union card. A broad functional orientation has spread widely. Perhaps there is reason to hope that a sociological approach will find an increasingly important place in anthropological research.

In the main, however, the sociologist has no reason to complain. He has used only a small part of the comparative material made available to him by anthropology for the testing of hypotheses concerning religion. If he can avoid the dangers of the pick and choose illustrative method by full awareness of the range of data, following the lead of Professor Murdock in this regard, he can use anthropological studies much more extensively than he has.

In summary, may I suggest that the principal contributions of anthropology to the sociology of religion have been indirect, but not, for that reason, any less important. Anthropology has kept alive, much more thoroughly than sociology, an interest in religion as an important part of the life of man. It has fought a persistent ethnocentrism by the stress on objective recording of, indeed even respect for, the data of all societies. It has greatly extended the possibilities of a comparative approach. And finally, anthropology has continually emphasized to the sociologist the need to see cultures as wholes, not fragments of unrelated parts. Without this perspective, an adequate sociology of religion is impossible.

FOOTNOTES

1. Yinger, J. Milton. *Religion, Society, and the Individual.* The Macmillan Company, 1957, pp. 20-21.
2. I shall disregard the interest in religion expressed in the work of Comte, Ward, and Ellwood. A large share of the emphasis of such writers is on sociology *as* religion (or a religious substitute) not a sociology of religion.
3. It perhaps should be noted that the influence has been reciprocal. Radcliffe-Brown was clearly influenced by Durkheim; and even Malinowski, despite the stronger individualism in his theory and his critique of Durkheim, seems to have drawn some of his functionalism from the French sociologist.
4. Merton, Robert K. *Social Theory and Social Structure.* Toward the Codification of Theory and Research, rev. ed., The Free Press, 1957, pp. 27-38.
5. Malinowski, Bronislaw. "Magic, Science, and Religion," in *Science, Religion and Reality,* Joseph Needham, ed. The Macmillan Company, 1925, pp. 49-50.
6. Hertzler, J. O. "Religious Institutions," *Annals of the American Academy of Political and Social Science,* March, 1948, pp. 1-13.
7. Davis, Kingsley. *Human Society.* The Macmillan Company, 1949, p. 532.
8. Fauset, Arthur Huff. *Black Gods of the Metropolis.* University of Pennsylvania Press, 1944, p. 81.
9. See Purnell H. Benson, *Religion in Contemporary Culture,* Harper & Brothers, 1960; Thomas F. Hoult, *The Sociology of Religion,* The Dryden Press, 1958; David O. Moberg, *The Church as a Social Institution,* Prentice-Hall, 1962; Glenn M. Vernon, *Sociology of Religion,* McGraw-Hill, 1962; and J. Milton Yinger, *Religion, Society and the Individual.*

In addition to the references in the footnotes, the following are some of the writings referred to or alluded to in this chapter.

Clark, Elmer T. *The Small Sects in America,* rev. ed. Abingdon-Cokesbury Press, 1949.

Durkheim, Emile. *The Elementary Forms of the Religious Life.* George Allen and Unwin, 1915.

Fromm, Erich. *Escape from Freedom.* Rinehart and Co., 1941.

Fromm, Erich. *Psychoanalysis and Religion*. Yale University Press, 1950.

Goode, William J. *Religion Among the Primitives*. The Free Press, 1951.

Howells, William W. *The Heathens: Primitive Man and His Religions*. Doubleday and Company, Inc., 1948.

Kirkpatrick, Clifford. *Religion in Human Affairs*. John Wiley and Sons, 1929.

Kroeber, A. L. *Anthropology*, rev. ed. Harcourt, Brace and Co., 1948.

Le Bras, Gabriel. *Etudes de Sociologie Religieuse*. Presses Universitaires de France, 1955.

Lowie, Robert H. *Primitive Religion*. Boni and Liveright, 1924.

Malinowski, Bronislaw. *The Foundations of Faith and Morals*. Oxford University Press, 1936.

Niebuhr, H. Richard. *The Social Sources of Denominationalism*. Henry Holt & Co., Inc., 1929.

Nottingham, Elizabeth. *Religion and Society*. Doubleday & Company, Inc., 1954.

Parsons, Talcott. *Essays in Sociological Theory Pure and Applied*. The Free Press, 1949.

Parsons, Talcott. *Religious Perspectives of College Teaching in Sociology and Social Psychology*. The Edward W. Hazen Foundation, New Haven, 1951.

Parsons, Talcott. *The Social System*. The Free Press, 1951.

Pin, Emile, *Pratique Religieuse et Classes Sociales*. Editions Spes, 1956.

Pope, Liston. *Millhands and Preachers*. Yale University Press, 1942.

Radcliffe-Brown, A. R. "On the Concept of Function in Social Science," *American Anthropologist*, 1935, vol. 37, pp. 394-402.

Radcliffe-Brown, A. R. "Religion and Society." Royal Anthropological Institute of Great Britain and Ireland, 1945.

Radin, Paul. *Primitive Religion, Its Nature and Origin*. The Viking Press, 1937.

Simpson, George E. "Jamaican Revivalist Cults," *Social and Economic Studies*, Dec., 1956.

Sklare, Marshall. *Conservative Judaism: An American Religious Movement*. The Free Press, 1955.

Swanson, Guy E. *The Birth of the Gods*. University of Michigan Press, 1960.

Tawney, R. H. *Religion and the Rise of Capitalism.* Harcourt, Brace and Co., 1926.

Troeltsch, Ernst. *The Social Teaching of the Christian Churches.* The Macmillan Company, 1931.

Vogt, Evon Z. and O'Dea, Thomas F. "A Comparative Study of the Role of Values in Social Action in Two Southwestern Communities," *American Sociological Review*, Dec., 1953, vol. 18, no. 6, pp. 645-654.

Wach, Joachim. *Sociology of Religion.* University of Chicago Press, 1944.

Warner, Wellman J. *The Wesleyan Movement in the Industrial Revolution.* Longmans, Green and Co., 1930.

Weber, Max. *The Protestant Ethic and the Spirit of Capitalism.* George Allen and Unwin, 1930.

Weber, Max. *The Religion of China.* The Free Press, 1951.

Williams, Robin M., Jr. *American Society.* Alfred Knopf, 1951.

Yinger, J. Milton. *Religion in the Struggle for Power. A Study in the Sociology of Religion.* Duke University Press, 1946.

6

Areas for Research
in the Sociology of Religion

CONTINUOUS INTERPLAY between research and theory is essential to the scientific method. Attempts to push one ahead of the other are likely to be relatively unrewarding: atheoretical research is disjointed and inadequately cumulative; theory that is not continually tested and revised by research is speculative and of unknown validity.

Through the years, the sociology of religion has been more extensively developed in its theoretical than in its research aspects. In the last ten or fifteen years, however, this situation has begun to change, with reports of field research appearing in increasing numbers. The task ahead is to accelerate this trend without a slackening of theoretical work. In fact, the continuing development of a scientific theory of religion now becomes both more possible and more essential in order to make maximum use of the richer materials.

It is the purpose of this chapter to outline the major research areas of the sociology of religion, to indicate a few of the advances that have been made in recent years, and to indicate some of the lines of development that seem to offer promise for future research. There will be no attempt, in this "stocktaking" report, to analyze individual contributions to the sociology of religion except as that is necessary to illustrate major trends.

Unfortunately, there are still important disagreements concerning the definition of the sociology of religion. This may be inevitable in a field which attracts the attention of students from many different disciplines and involves significant value perspectives. But such disagreement blocks communication and advance in the field. Realizing that definitions are not "right" or "wrong" but are to be judged by their usefulness, and realizing that no one has a "monopoly" on a term—others may define sociology of religion differently—I will designate research areas in terms of the definition given in the preceding chapter. That statement implies that the sociology of religion is a branch of scientific sociology; it is not a marginal field between theology and sociology; religion is the datum and sociology the method of approach. The sociology of religion is nonvaluative, objective, and abstract. It studies empirical phenomena to try to isolate generalizations concerning the interconnections of religious behavior with other social behavior.

This definition may become clearer if I indicate one or two things which the sociology of religion is not. If the sociology of religion is a science, interested in the typical and attempting to develop generalizations that will enable it to predict, then it is not simply the "social history" of religion—that is, the history of the more purely secular aspects of religious groups or the history of the relationship between religious institutions and other parts of the social structure. Indeed, it is not history at all. That is not to say that church historians and others concerned with describing the place of religion in society have not made valuable contributions to the sociology of religion. They have added to our store of data, have given us concepts of value, and have frequently offered insights and hypotheses that are well worth testing. Nor is the sociology of religion the story of the development of "the social gospel" (a definition in harmony with the idea that sociology is the study of social problems). Some of the literature on "Christian sociology" gives the impression, seldom explicitly stated, that such a definition is used. Both the study of the "social history" of religious groups and the study of "the social gospel" give data which may be of great value to the sociologist of religion, but they raise different kinds of questions. While the student of the "social gospel" may ask, "What have religious groups done to interest themselves in international conflict, slum conditions, race relations, trade-union activities, child labor, etc.?" the sociologist of religion will ask, "What do certain kinds of religious groups *typically* do when social change produces dislocations or when the moral teachings of religion tend to come into conflict with some of the interests of powerful classes in society?" The two questions may deal with the same data. The student of the social history of religion may ask: "What was the relation between the church and the secular powers in the fifteenth century in Italy?" The sociologist of religion asks: "Do these data tell us anything of how certain kinds of religious groups tend to relate themselves to the political structures and political changes of their time?"

Needless to say, the sociology of religion gives a very incomplete picture of the total meaning of religion in the life of man. A complete picture would require not only the additions of other objective or "external" studies, psychology and history, for example, but also the kinds of evaluative study that come from theology and aesthetics. I have no desire to quarrel with those who consider the sociology of religion an unimportant aspect of the total view. The desirability of science, after all, is a value stand itself and cannot be defended on scientific grounds.

I. The Requisites for a Sound Sociology of Religion

The sociology of religion requires a group of integrated and testable propositions, harmonious with the larger theoretical schemes of general sociology. This demands that hypotheses be made explicit and be posed in such a way that they can be tested by empirical work. Some of the ingredients for this kind of study are at hand; but the systematic interrelation of all the component parts is manifest in only a small part of the studies with which I am familiar. In an analysis of the sociology of knowledge (a discipline which overlaps more or less—depending on how one defines "knowledge"—with the sociology of religion) Robert Merton calls attention to the contrast between the European and the American studies in the field. Although the distinction he draws between European and American work seems less appropriate today than when Merton wrote, the contrast still deserves study, because it indicates clearly the need for bringing theoretical and empirical work together. European sociology of knowledge, Merton says, "belongs for the most part to the camp of global theorists, in which the breadth and significance of the problem justifies one's dedication to it, sometimes quite apart from the present possibility of materially advancing beyond ingenious speculations and impressionistic conclusions. By and large, the sociologists of knowledge have been among those raising high the banner which reads, 'We don't know that what we say is true, but it is at least significant.' " [1] American students have been more interested in canvassing mass opinions. They have been concerned with getting representative samples of opinion, recorded on objectified scales. Their motto might be: "We don't know that what we say is particularly significant, but it is at least true." [2]

This difference in approach influences the judgments of what are facts and data that can be useful for scientific study—with the European scholar, in most instances, ready to accept a wider range of material. If an author has high intellectual status, his impressions, Merton points out, are often taken for facts. If this is true in Mannheim's sociology of knowledge, it is certainly no less true in Joachim Wach's sociology of religion, where generalizations are frequently supported by reference to the writings of "the outstanding scholar" in the field. The same "tolerance" for somewhat questionable "facts" is also found in the work of Max Weber, despite his brilliant mastery of the logic of science. He built his theories of the relationship between religious ethics and economic behavior, for example, partly on his judgment that the nonreligious factors in China of the sixteenth and seventeenth centuries were as favorable to the rise of capitalism as were the nonreligious factors in Western Europe. This judgment of an enormously complex theoretical problem was based on examination of the few score written records—with very little possibility for checking them for reliability and completeness. The present writer must confess—and thereby apply a little of sociology of knowledge to himself —that such research is insufficiently empirical for his American taste. Although highly insightful and stimulating, this kind of sociology of religion, trying to solve theoretical problems that are too large at this stage of development of the field, is almost completely lacking in propositions that can be put in the form of testable hypotheses. (Many Weber scholars will disagree sharply with this—pointing to the way in which he "thought away" variables. A discussion of this methodological problem would take us beyond the limits of this volume.)

American sociology of knowledge (and, I continue to add, sociology of religion), on the other hand, asks first whether or not a given observation is true, and only later, if at all, asks about its theoretical significance. This "leads prematurely to a curbing of imaginative hypotheses." [8] If this is true of the flood of opinion studies, it is no less true of the great bulk of the studies on city churches, sectarian beliefs and practices, and church histories which make up the raw materials of a sociology of religion in the United States. The need in both fields, of course, is to bring the theoretical and empirical emphases into close and fruitful interaction. That has happened all too rarely in the sociology of religion, and it may be helpful to try to discover the reasons. These two factors seem to be involved.

First, competent research in the sociology of religion demands a combination of skills and interests that is not very common. In fact, there are some ways in which the necessary elements are mutually contradictory. The researcher must, in the first place, have a thoroughly adequate grasp of contemporary sociological theory and research methods. He must be entirely objective in his handling of the data of religion; yet he must be strongly interested in the material and deeply acquainted with it. Among sociologists there are persons who consider themselves "religious," others who are "antireligious," and still others who are largely indifferent to religion. Those in the first two groups very often lack the objectivity, and those in the last group lack the interest, in developing a sociology of religion. Those who undertake studies in the sociology of religion without a mastery of sociological theory and methodology, on the other hand, may make many useful and accurate observations, but they will often fail to add to the sociology of religion as I have defined it, because they structure their problems in a different way. This difficulty sometimes mars, for example, the excellent work of Joachim Wach, *Sociology of Religion*.

Second, despite the almost inexhaustible supply of data on primitive and civilized religions, on church history, on sectarian movements, and the vast supply of religious materials in written form—sermons, official publications of church bodies, and so forth—there is really a scarcity of empirical material out of which to fashion adequate generalizations. It is very difficult to judge the reliability of much of the data. Many of the accounts of the religious practices of primitive people are the observations of one person only, completely unchecked by other researchers. Elaborate theories in the sociology of religion have been built on historical records two or three or twenty-five centuries old, where the problem of checking reliability and particularly the problem of checking completeness are overwhelming. That does not mean that highly significant hypotheses cannot grow from the examination of such material but only that definitive conclusions are unwarranted. Basing conclusions on the religious beliefs of a time, for example, on surviving written beliefs, is highly inadequate. Documents that were written at the time being studied often omit the most common facts, because they are taken for granted; while those written later, which try to fill in the gaps, contain the perspectives of the writer and of his time. We need not completely agree with Voltaire—that history is a group of tricks we play on the dead—to recognize the difficulties in building a scientific sociology of religion on historical materials. Why some beliefs were written down and others not is a very important problem for the sociology of religion; and, of those beliefs that were written, why some survived and others did not is equally important. But by the very nature of the case, these things cannot be known for Greece of the fourth century B.C. or for Calvin's Geneva.

Many of the data available for use by the sociologist of religion, moreover, are lacking in comparability. This greatly hinders a study that is trying to discover generalizations. A related problem is that data which were gathered without the guidance of explicit scientific concepts are often of limited usefulness for scientific purposes. Ideally, empirical materials are gathered in direct reference to testable hypotheses. Very few of the data with which sociologists of religion have been working satisfy this requirement. (It is clear, of course, that there are important scientific dangers involved in this use of a hypothesis. These dangers, however, are scarcely to be avoided by falling into raw empiricism or by using data that were gathered under the "guidance" of some other hypothesis —implicit or explicit—than the one used by the researcher. The danger is to be met by making the hypothesis more explicit and more tentative.)

II. Some Research Areas in the Sociology of Religion

The areas for research listed here are neither mutually exclusive nor exhaustive. They are fields in which vital beginnings have been made or which seem to me to be of importance in the development of the sociology of religion. I believe that testable hypotheses can be worked out in each of these areas, although adequate work in some of them is dependent upon the accumulation of data over many years. At the present time, comparisons through time are unreliable, because information for earlier periods is sketchy and often noncomparable.

The broadest area for research is the comparative study of religious variation in different types of societies. How do religious beliefs and practices vary with the nature of the economy, with the rapidity of social change, with the level of literacy, with the methods of socialization, with the types of stratification systems, and the like? What happens to a religion when a group of its adherents migrate to another society of substantially different type from their homeland? Comparisons may be between different societies or they may refer to one society at different times. Although Weber's classic studies of the interconnections of religion and economic activity took the lead in using the comparative approach, only recently has it ben used with any regularity.[4]

Cross-cultural comparative studies are closely related to the analysis of relationships between religion and other aspects of a social structure. I can only suggest the vast range of research problems in this area by noting some of the questions that may be raised. With respect to religion and the family: How do different family patterns interact with religion? Does decline in the size and solidarity of the family affect religious training, the continuity of tradition, the religious tendencies of the persons involved? How do the different roles of men and of women affect their religious inclinations? How are religious beliefs and practices related to the sexual ethics of various societies? What are the factors that block or permit interfaith marriage, and with what results? Under what conditions will family cults and ancestor worship become a part of a religious system?

There are equally important questions involved in the study of the connection between religion and education and the related problem of religion and science. How do religions vary in their congeniality for the growth of knowledge and science? What are the effects on the pursuit of knowledge when education is under religious control or is distinctively secular? More specifically, how does education in various parochial schools in the United States affect the aspirations, the values, and other tendencies of the individuals involved when compared with the influence of secular public schools? There are obvious difficulties in setting up a study of this question in such a way that "other things are equal," but close approximations of good design are possible.[5]

In many societies, to share a political allegiance is to share a religious perspective; the boundaries of the political and religious communities are coterminous. This is clearly not the case in most modern societies. A number of the most important research problems for the sociology of religion emerge from the separation of religion and citzenship. Under what conditions does religion support and when does it restrict nationalistic sentiments? How are various messianic movements related to the emerging nationalism of colonial peoples? Are religious movements and political movements functional alternatives or are they likely to be found together? There is good evidence that political perspectives are affected by religion within nations as well as in cross-national comparisons, even when such other variables as education and class are controlled. Lenski found that Catholics whose socioeconomic position was upper-middle class, in many respects shared the perspectives of working-class people because of their involvement in a Catholic subcommunity which was predominantly working class. It is difficult, in research in this area, to equate all other variables (recency with which class standing was established, friends and relatives in other classes, occupational differences, and so on) in order to eliminate spurious correlations, but the problem is an important one.[6]

A broader question in this area is concerned with the causes and effects of various kinds of relationship between religious institutions and the state. There is a vast literature on the question of "church and state," most of it historical in approach, and much of it polemical. It may be that the problem is too large for adequate scientific work. Certainly full attention must be paid to the many different kinds of religious groups and kinds of states involved— one cannot talk about *the* relationship between church and state. The consequences of connection between church and state in England (Established Church), Spain (Catholic Church), Russia (Reestablished Church), and Japan (prewar Shinto) are clearly of very different orders.

Perhaps we can focus attention on this problem by proposing a hypothesis: In a society with highly centralized state power, the religious groups tend to be subservient to the state whether or not there exists a formal institutional connection; or, in *times* when the state becomes the central locus of power (for example, during war or cold war), church and state become highly interrelated. Whether or not a church is "established" is less significant —in terms of its place in society—than the structure of power of the society within which it works. In societies where, from a democratic point of view, it is most desirable to separate church and state, it is least possible to do so. If I may inject a value position, Protestants who fight the use of public-school buses to take children to parochial schools while they accept, and even encourage, the trend toward the nationalization of Christianity that is so characteristic of our time are choking on a gnat and swallowing a camel. (Incidentally, I'm against swallowing gnats.) Both in scientific and in value terms, the significant relationships between church and state are not only the formal ones, the ones easily described by institutional structure, but also the pervasive, informal interaction. This is not to say that the institutionalization of a church-state relationship does not affect it. I am noting simply that the structural element is not the only factor involved.

With the appearance of societies containing adherents of several religions, the problem of religious conflict arose. Even earlier, of course, religious conflict, entangled in complex ways with economic and political conflict, had arisen between societies. One of the key questions in this area is to discover the degree to which religion is the substance of the dispute and the degree to which it is simply the symbol of other disputes. How religious were the religious wars of Christendom? Was the split of Pakistan and India based substantially on religious conflict? To what degree is a religious factor involved in Arab-Israeli tensions today? More manageable questions emerge from the study of religious conflict within a nation. Here the task is to discover the conditions under which antipathy, tolerance, active mediation, and amalgamation occur among religious groups. What factors led, in the United States, to the National Conference of Christians and Jews and what factors promote the Ku Klux Klan? Several recent studies have extended our knowledge of religious conflict.[7]

The relationship between economic interests and religion quickly comes to attention as the result of the study of conflict. This relationship has probably been studied more extensively than any other aspect of the sociology of religion. Does a religion, by the influence of its road to salvation, its interpretation of work, its particular combination of values, help to create the situation within which economic activities are pursued; or does it merely reflect economic forces? More accurately, under what conditions and to what degree does each of these relationships prevail? How is religion involved in the production, distribution, and consumption of wealth?

An area of research closely related both to the study of conflict and to the study of economic-religious interaction is the exploration of the relationship between religious differentiation and social stratification. These three themes, in fact, often occur together. It is well known that in socially differentiated societies, the various secular groups tend to exhibit differences in doctrine, worship, and religious group structure. Religious variation is related to differences in style of life among the several strata, because aspirations, values, aesthetic patterns, emotional needs, and so forth—which vary to some degree by class—all affect religious inclinations. The distinction between church and sect, developed by Troeltsch and Weber, is based largely on observation of this fact. Yet it must be pointed out that under some circumstances the correlation between class status, for example, and religious group association, is far from perfect. There are some forces that tend to divide people religiously according to class, but there are other forces that divide them along other lines and still others that tend to unite a differentiated group into one religious community. These forces obscure one another. Women in all classes may share, for example, a similar status in many respects; and this status may give them a common religious tendency that cuts across the different religious tendencies they get from their different class statuses. When one adds just a few other differentiating factors such as rural or urban residence, amount of education, and so on, one sees that any easy attempt to classify religious groups solely on the basis of class is bound to be inadequate. Keeping in mind the need for avoiding any oversimplified picture of the relationship between social differentiation and religious differentiation, one can nevertheless use this problem as an important approach to the sociology of religion. Liston Pope, for example, writes:

Religious beliefs as well as practices are profoundly affected by the special problems inhering in the social and economic status of mill workers. Their religion is intimately related to the everyday struggles and vicissitudes of an insecure life, and proves useful for interpretation and for succor. It "works" and "changes things." . . . Attempt at summary of the satisfactions he (the millworker) finds in his church points to economic influences even more clearly. In general terms, he derives two benefits: the organization of life, and the transvaluation of life. . . . Less exclusively than in rural areas, but more largely than in uptown districts, the church in the mill village is a community center; in the comparative absence of other social institutions, it is the focal point around which noneconomic life in the village largely revolves. Naturally leaders among the workers find in it almost their only vehicle for expression of leadership. . . . But the worker also looks to his church to find transvaluation of life, which may take the form of reassurance or of escape, or both. By affirmation of values denied in the economic world, the church provides comfort and ultimate assurance; in its religious services it often affords escape temporarily from the economic and social situation in which workaday life must be spent. The difficulties of life for the mill worker in this world help to explain the noteworthy emphasis on otherworldliness in his churches.[8]

A central thesis of this study is that social differentiation finds its counterpart (not without complicating factors) in religious differentiation. A long series of studies gives indication of the fruitfulness of this approach in the sociology of religion. Pre-Reformation sects, the Reformation itself, the rise of Quakerism and Methodism, the denomination-forming process in the United States and Canada, and the religious groupings of minority groups have been interpreted as, in part, religious expressions of secular conflicts and social distinctions. This can be understood partly in terms of different personality needs and tendencies, but in part it reflects the way in which secular differences invade the religious sphere to get support for secular battles. During the strikes of 1877 the *Congregationalist* declared:

Bring on then the troops—the armed police—in overwhelming numbers. Bring out the Gatling guns. Let there be no fooling with blank cartridges. But let the mob know, everywhere, that for it to stand one moment after it has been ordered by proper authorities to disperse, will be to be shot down in its tracks. . . . A little of the vigor of the first Napoleon is the thing we need now. Compromise would simply sow the wind for "future whirlwind reaping." [9]

It is unlikely that the workingmen involved in trying to establish a trade union would look upon such "religion"—and the institutions in which it was embodied—with enthusiasm.

We discussed in Chapter Two some of the ways in which religious doctrines and movements are involved in the struggles of those who are low in status and power. This is well shown in Winstanley's words:

True religion and undefiled is this, to make restitution of the Earth which hath been taken and held from the common people.[10] . . . At this very day poor people are forced to work for 4d. a day, and corn is dear. And the tithing-priest stops their mouth, and tells them that "inward satisfaction of mind" was meant by the declaration "The poor shall inherit the earth." I tell you, the scripture is to be really and materially fulfilled. . . . You jeer at the name Leveller. I tell you Jesus Christ is the head Leveller.[11]

In contrast to this statement of Winstanley's, sectarian groups probably develop an escapist doctrine more often than a doctrine which directly challenges the secular powers. One of the largest gaps in this area of the sociology of religion is the determination of the conditions under which a religious group will accept the secular order, "withdraw" from society by devaluing it, or challenge and attack the secular power structure. The nature of the religious tradition out of which the sectarian movement grows, the chance of success in the secular world, the presence or absence of more strictly secular institutions trying to change the *status quo*, the tendencies of the leadership, the availability of governmental channels for registering protests, and other variables would have to be considered.

The opposite side of the hypothesis we have been discussing has been examined much less often. How does religious differentiation, once established, affect social differentiation? Does it tend to fix social divisions, or does it only reflect them? We know that, when some of the social factors for the religious division have disappeared, there tends to be a reunion (for example, the Methodist movement, 1840-1940). But what consequences grow out of the lag? Does the experience of being brought up in close touch with a "lower-class" church tend to give one values, levels of aspiration, and motives that fix one in lower-class status? It was once thought that the sect-to-church transition disproved this; that, as John Wesley declared, the virtues that went along with religious fervor helped one to climb the class ladder. Now some evidence casts doubt on this idea; the transition from sect to church may be characteristic of the institution only and not be indicative of what is happening to the status of individual members. If churches become middle class in values, doctrine, and ritual, lower-class members tend to drop out and to look for some other religious (or secular) expression more in keeping with their desires.[12] On the other hand, the religious association may promote discipline, thrift, and leadership training, thus contributing to the chances of upward social mobility. A major task is to measure the influence of these opposite forces. The effects of religious differentiation on social differentiation are not beyond the reach of scientific research, but analysis requires the extensive longitudinal study (of a generation or more) for which social science is as yet poorly prepared.

Finally, it should be observed, with regard to the hypothesis under discussion, that the role of religion in *reducing* social differentiation—in unifying a society—has often been discussed. This is central in the work of Durkheim and receives an interesting formulation in Wach's study, where he distinguishes between situations where religion and natural groups are coterminous and situations where specifically religious groups have developed. Again, the need is for careful specification of the *conditions under which* the unifying influences of religion are operative and those under which the differentiating influences are operative.

Springing readily from the issues involved in the study of the interrelations of religion, economics, conflict, and stratification is the analysis of religion and social change. Since I have dealt with this theme at many points in the preceding chapters, I will bring it into this listing of major research areas simply by stating two well known hypotheses.

The rise of Holiness and Pentecostal churches in the southeastern United States "is largely the natural product of the social disorganization and cultural conflict which have attended the overrapid urbanward migration and concomitant urbanization of an intensely rural, and among other things, religiously fundamentalist population." [13]

To put this in terms of a more general theoretical proposition, one might say: When a religiously fundamentalist group living in a society of free religious choice migrates from a fairly isolated and stable community into a mobile, impersonal one, they will tend to join or create religious groups that help to reestablish a communal feeling, that declare unambiguous standards of behavior, that bolster the feeling of importance—very often by an otherworldly emphasis. Variables to control include differing individual personality tendencies, the degree of communal and associational character of the two settings (this is a continuum, not a dichotomy), the proportion of the population of a community made up of migrants, the availability of alternative modes of adjustment (for example, trade unions), etc.

"The religious valuation of restless, continuous, systematic work in a worldly calling, as the highest means to asceticism, and at the same time the surest and most evident proof of rebirth and genuine faith, must have been the most powerful conceivable lever for the expansion of that attitude toward life which we have here called the spirit of capitalism." [14] This is perhaps the best-known hypothesis in the sociology of religion. It expresses Weber's belief that Protestant asceticism, particularly Calvinism, was highly influential in the appearance of the capitalist spirit. His data are not only the writings and activities of churchmen but the high correlation between Calvinist belief and the particular kind of capitalistic behavior he is talking about. The emphasis in his essay on the *interaction* between ideas and "material conditions," is of great value. Weber's study is not, however, without serious difficulties of which the sociologist of religion needs to be fully aware. It shares the problems of large-scale historical sociology—selectivity of material and the difficulty of checking reliability. Weber, in seeking to supplement one-sided materialistic theories, skipped over too lightly the way in which Calvin himself, trying to be effective in semicommercial

Geneva, was partially shaped by emerging capitalism. A central problem in the sociology of knowledge and religion is that of the "audience": the group to whom one addresses himself, in speaking or writing, influences, by its values and needs, the problems one sets for himself, the emphases, even the criteria of validity. In other words, spoken and written ideas that survive are not so "immanent" (a very slippery concept in Weber's work) as he indicated, for they go through a process of winnowing strongly influenced by the "audience" involved. Weber also failed to take sufficient theoretical account of the importance of the great changes in Calvinism over a period of two or three centuries. His own concept of "elective affinity" puts a different light on the causal relationship of Calvinism to the spirit of capitalism. This is not to deny, however, that religious ideas have a measure of independent development (their own inner dialectic, as Troeltsch would say), and that, once established, they influence the activities of those who hold them. Wherever Calvinism's emphasis on "this-worldly asceticism" came from, it seems highly likely that a child brought up believing in it and socialized to its values, would, if he as an adult became involved in capitalist economic activities, approach them in a different spirit from one whose value orientations were of a different order, toward, for example, sharp denial of the importance of success in this world, or away from asceticism. Despite the difficulty of testing it, Weber's theory gets a measure of support, when properly qualified, from its harmony with other work that is capable of empirical testing. Perhaps the major contribution of Weber's hypothesis, however, is the stimulation it gave to further work. Controversy has surrounded it from the beginning—both because of value questions involved and because of the great difficulties of empirical tests. Some have accepted it with minor qualifications (Troeltsch and Parsons), some have utterly disagreed (Robertson and Samuelsson), some have criticized it sharply but commended its insights (Tawney), and some have agreed with the idea that a religious force was behind capitalism but declared that it was other than Protestantism (Sombart and Fanfani).

It is clear from these examples, and many others that we might cite, that it is very difficult to isolate a purely religious influence in social change, because religious institutions and movements contain many nonreligious elements and secular institutions and movements are often led by persons with religiously derived interests and supported by persons with religiously influenced values.

Another major area of research deals with the kinds of relationship to be found between religion and morals. This is an area where it is peculiarly difficult to state hypotheses in a way that permits testing. Because of the great importance of the problem, however, continued effort to do so seems appropriate. The question first entered the sociology of religion in connection with theories of the origin of religion. Several interpretations, all hypothetical reconstructions from too little data, vie for acceptance. One group of writers holds that in its earlier stages, and in its origins, religion had no connection with morals. The common element in several different theories, among which I shall not take time to draw distinctions, is that religion (in the first instance) is a product of insecurity and fear. Buffeted by natural forces, plagued by illness, dismayed by the fact of death, the human mind created a "compensation ideology" to reduce the insecurity. Am I powerless to assure my food supply, to cure illness, to avoid death? Then I shall (perhaps unconsciously) posit the existence of a power that can do these things; and I shall only have to learn how to get and keep that power on my side. Such a belief can reduce tensions, overcome fear, and even pragmatically "prove" itself, because it produces greater courage, coordination, and patience. Only later, this theory goes on to state, do moral elements become associated with religion. The development of the

Hebrew conception of God from a tribal deity of vengeance and wrath to a universal God of love is perhaps the classic illustration of this idea. The precise ways in which the experiences of the Jews affected this development are questions of great interest—but of even greater difficulty. The hypothesis that defeat, bondage, and culture contact were important factors is plausible. At any rate, by the eighth century B.C. we see an ethical God who cared not for gifts but for repentance: "I hate, I despise your feasts," says Yahweh, "and I take no delight in your solemn assemblies. Even though you offer me your burnt offerings and cereal offerings, I will not accept them, and the peace offerings of your fatted beasts I will not look upon. . . . But let justice roll down like waters, and righteousness like an overflowing stream."

Another theory holds that religion and morals must be seen as emerging together—that beliefs and cultic practices are, in essence, the reflection of community solidarity and moral unity. Religion is a kind of projection, on a cosmic screen, of the tribal organization and the moral order. Durkheim writes:

So everything leads us back to this same idea: before all, rites are means by which the social group reaffirms itself periodically. From this, we may be able to reconstruct hypothetically, the way in which the totemic cult [which Durkheim considered the "elementary form of religious life"] should have risen originally. Men who feel themselves united, partially by bonds of blood, but still more by a community of interest and tradition, assemble and become conscious of their moral unity.[15]

Whatever theory may, ultimately, seem most adequate to describe the origin of the relationship between religion and morals, the effects of their relationship deserve careful study. We can focus our attention on this problem by stating a hypothesis. In a highly dynamic society, the belief that morality is a fixed pattern of behavior "revealed" to man as one aspect of his religion, and in an important sense, therefore, subservient to his religion, is a belief that makes moral behavior *less* likely. The problem is stated in this way, not because there is much evidence to support it, but because an "outrageous hypothesis" may have value in jolting us into a fresh examination of a problem of high significance that has been largely neglected. Most people would state the hypothesis oppositely: that a moral code unsupported by the sanctions of religion would be difficult to enforce, that the more strenuous demands of morality, at any rate, would not be heeded were it not for their religious color. I must confess to an almost complete lack of data to test the first (or second) hypothesis; but it could be stated in such a way as to be amenable to empirical study: Define morality operationally and objectively; then measure the relationship in the behavior of persons who have been matched for such variables as age, education, income, and so forth, between "morality score" and belief that the moral code is a fixed part of revealed religion. If those with the higher morality scores were those who were least inclined to look upon their moral code as a fixed item of their religion, the hypothesis would be supported.[16]

My reasoning, if such it be, in suggesting such a heretical hypothesis and in believing that it might have some research value, is somewhat as follows: The idea that morality is a fixed item of religious belief attaches a static quality to morality and religion that weakens them both, in a rapidly changing society. One dare not challenge outmoded religious beliefs for fear of weakening the moral code which those beliefs supposedly bolster; and, on the other hand, one dare not question an inadequate moral code because it seems to be an attack upon religious absolutes. In the modern world, where the need for continually revising some aspects of both morality and religion is great, this rigidity weakens both. In the field of morals there has been a great lag in developing a code of behavior that is appropriate to the urban, mobile, secondary world in which so many of us live. To a significant degree we literally do not know how to behave. We are equipped with standards of morality which help us to adjust to the face-to-face contacts of a communal relationship (the kind of setting in which our moral code developed) but which leave us much less well instructed about the moral problems that arise from the fact that we deal with strangers more than with friends, that we affect hundreds whom we do not know. A man may support the church, love his wife, befriend his neighbors, and then manufacture a patent drug which cheats millions and perhaps injures thousands. And our society does not know whether to call him a smart businessman or a scoundrel. To tell him to treat all men as his neighbors is somewhat ambiguous advice at best, and it fails to recognize that neighborly morality had a kind of reciprocal enforcement arrangement, growing from daily face-to-face contact. An effective moral code for modern urban life would tell a man, not how he ought to act toward neighbors alone, but also how he ought to act toward strangers, toward people whom he will never see or know about, but whom he will affect in this highly interdependent and specialized society. It would indicate the important role of social institutions, and other social mechanisms in affecting social interaction, instead of emphasizing that a "right heart" alone is necessary to moral behavior.

The hypothesis also suggests that the assumption that moral standards are simply one phase of revealed religion also has important consequences for religion, for such an assumption helps to prevent the continuing development of religious thought which is necessary if religion is to remain vital. There is a constant need for the shuffling off of accidental and outworn religious beliefs and practices—the traditional elements—in order that the intrinsic elements may flourish. Many Christians cling to magical and superstitious elements in religion for fear that, if they are challenged, the edifice of morality which they are supposed to support will come tumbling down. If one starts from the premise that the body of specific religious beliefs that he happens to hold are true—purely and simply, without any possibility of challenge—then the above argument is entirely without force. If, however, one assumes that the "truth" of religion is something for which man is continually striving, but never attaining, that religion is to be judged by its consequences, that it is in man, and not apart from him, that it reflects his fears and aspirations—then the problem we are discussing in this section becomes highly significant both in terms of values and in terms of a sociology of religion.

If one takes the latter view, he recognizes that religion is an ancient phenomenon which, because of the deeply emotional qualities associated with it, has been especially slow in casting off the elements that became associated with it in its early days. The conception of religion is an organic, changing thing (not simply development from "inferior" types to "my" religion, but continuous development within every religion) would lead one to say that the value of religion does not necessarily reside in the preservation of modes of thought which dominated the lives of primitive and ancient peoples. To be religious today, according to this conception, does not require that one think like an Australian aborigine, or an ancient Greek, or a thirteenth-century monk or even a Calvin or a Wesley—although most people assume that it does.

Another aspect of my reasoning in posing the hypothesis stated above is concerned with the way in which religious sanctions have been used by powerful people to hold or increase their power. The ruling classes of all societies have discovered that, when correctly used, religion can be a very effective weapon for them. For, however and whenever it occurred, once the idea that religion was involved, not only in man's relationship to higher powers, but also in man's relationship to his fellowmen, a *double-edged* sword was forged that has not always served the masses of men well. Not only could supernatural sanctions be used to enforce the moral code, but the same halo of sanctity could serve to give protection to any power structure, provided only that it had the power to control the definitions of "the moral" and "the good." Thus "religion" can say that to buy and sell slaves is part of the good society; that the czarist regime of 1915 is sacrosanct; that the Italian attack on Abyssinia is blessed; that child labor in the mills is a brace to character; that the existing distribution of power and income in a given society is necessary to the good life (and that those who oppose such a pattern, therefore, attack not just a human power structure but divine law).

E. A. Ross once wrote that the *wise* men of society disguised their sociology as ethics and then went further to disguise their ethics as religion, not leaving to the "purblind many" the complicated task of figuring out what was best for all. One might with as much truth say that the *powerful* men of society have often disguised (even from themselves) their ambitions as ethics and their ethics as religion, thus to give a sacred face to that very secular struggle for income, power, and prestige which characterizes most societies. According to the hypothesis under discussion, the conception that morality is simply one phase of revealed religion makes this kind of thing more possible. A more highly self-conscious, flexible relationship between religion and morals would reduce its likelihood.

Because of the controversial and tentative nature of these statements, it is perhaps well to state again that the writer looks upon them only as a hypothesis—a preliminary guess at the truth. They are perhaps useful in focusing research attention but are not tested theories.

It is quite likely that the opposite hypothesis, stated briefly above—that religious sanctions strengthen the moral code—is also true under certain conditions. It is the task of the sociology of religion to describe the conditions which tend to bring about the first relationship and those that tend to encourage the second. Some of the other hypotheses we have mentioned may be useful in this regard.

Several of the research areas so far discussed have individual as well as group dimensions. These can be made explicit by asking: What are the personality functions of religion; in what various ways does religion become connected with, express, and influence the tensions, fears, anxieties, hopes, and aspirations of individuals? Although this is a social-psychological and not a general sociological question, it is closely connected with several other questions we have raised. Emphasis is shifted, however, from group process and structure to personality tendencies in stated situations.

Advances in social psychology are furnishing both empirical and theoretical foundations on which to build analyses of religious behavior. In addition, there is a noticeable trend toward integration of research and theory in cultural anthropology, sociology, and social psychology that promises a much more adequate theoretical framework for religious studies. The wide swings from rationalism to romanticism, from instinctivism to environmentalism, have been greatly reduced, if not eliminated. In the writer's judgment, the broad outlines of an integrated approach are laid down in the "field theory" of Kurt Lewin and J. F. Brown and in the interdisciplinary and cross-cultural studies of such men as Talcott Parsons, Ralph Linton, and Clyde Kluckhohn. I cannot undertake an analysis of the development here more than to state that it seeks to understand behavior as a result of interaction between individuals, with myriad tendencies but no fixed responses, and various kinds of sociocultural and physical situations. As Gardner Murphy puts it:

We cannot define the situation operationally except in reference to the specific organism which is involved; we cannot define the organism operationally, in such a way as to obtain predictive power for behavior, except in reference to the situation. Each serves to define the other; they are definable operationally while in the organism-situation field.[17]

Such an approach may lead to a theoretical system within which more adequate studies of the personality functions of religion can be carried on.

The problems in this area have stimulated a great deal of commentary, with references, for example, to the hypothesis that the origins of religion and changes in religion can partly be understood as efforts to adjust to fear and insecurity. When a satisfactory "definition" of critical life-events is disturbed or destroyed, many religious movements will arise to try to reestablish a sense of security (and, one might add, many nonreligious movements, sharing elements in common with religion, will also arise to try to solve the same problems). This hypothesis, expressed in many ways, has been stated over and over again. It is probably the explanation most frequently used by anthropologists to account for the phenomena of primitive religions and is scarcely less frequently applied to contemporary religious movements. It is difficult to frame this hypothesis in such a way as to permit empirical testing, so that our knowledge in the field remains somewhat tentative; yet comparative studies lend it a good deal of weight.

Malinowski found that two closely related tribes among the Trobriand Islanders had very different approaches to their common task of fishing. One tribe fished largely in inland waters and lagoons; they were seldom unsuccessful and rarely endangered. They pursued their work with a matter-of-factness that had little room for precautionary ritual. The other tribe fished in the open sea. Their catch was much less certain and the hazards far greater. Around their work they had woven an elaborate web of rite and ceremony whose function it was to rid them of insecurity, to placate unknown forces that constantly threatened their success. It seems a plausible explanation that their institutionalized religious forms were related to their economic and personal fears and anxieties.

When Europeans overran and destroyed much of the culture of the American Indians, enormous problems of social disorganization and personal confusion inevitably arose. The average Indian, with his culture discredited, his leaders made helpless, his old mode of life made impossible, became thoroughly disorganized. Efforts to "Christianize" him often produced a strange blend of pseudo-Christianity which reflected his personal needs as well as the group struggle. In some accounts, Hiawatha, the famous Iroquois sachem, and Jesus become blurred and blended into an Indian savior who will drive the white man from the continent. The Ghost Dance among the Plains Indians, discussed briefly in Chapter Two, can be read almost as a running psychoanalysis of their fears and hatreds, clothed in religious terms. The fact that some Indian tribes were much more susceptible to the cult of the Dance furnishes a kind of control group for testing the hypothesis that this religious innovation is a product of the fears, tensions, and frustrations of the Indians. It appears, in fact, that the tribes whose cultures had been least disrupted (for example, the Pueblos) were indifferent to the Ghost Dance, while those whose cultural integration had been most completely broken (for example, the Sioux) took it up with enormous enthusiasm. Before this simple comparison could be held to be a proof of the hypothesis, many other variables would have to be controlled—for example, degree of contact with the shamans or others who were teaching the new religious ideas, response of native leadership, congeniality of different cultures for this kind of religious expression, et cetera. Tentatively, however, the material at hand seems to support the hypothesis.

I have time here only for a brief listing of some of the ways in which this hypothesis has been examined with reference to ancient and modern groups. It is involved in Gilbert Murray's classic analysis of the "failure of nerve" of the post-Aristotelian Greeks. Erich Fromm uses it to explain the rise and spread of Lutheranism and Calvinism in early modern times. Hadley Cantril and others use it in their studies of the followers of Father Divine. It has an important place in Liston Pope's analysis of the religion of Southern mill villagers. It would be interesting to compare and contrast some of these religious movements with more secular movements to discover the similarities and differences in personality tendencies found among the various groups of searchers for a formula.

A brief statement of Fromm's analysis will indicate the way in which this hypothesis has been used to try to explain even a major religious development. Social and economic changes by the time of the sixteenth century had brought individual freedom not only from earlier economic and political forms but also freedom from ties that had furnished a sense of security. As Fromm says:

Life has ceased to be lived in a closed world the center of which was man; the world has become limitless and at the same time threatening. By losing his fixed place in a closed world man loses the answer to the meaning of life; the result is that doubt has befallen him concerning himself and the aim of life. He is threatened by powerful supra-personal forces, capital and the market. His relationship to his fellow men, with everyone a potential competitor, has become hostile and estranged; he is free—that is, he is alone, isolated, threatened from all sides. . . . The new freedom is bound to create a deep feeling of insecurity, powerlessness, doubt, aloneness, and anxiety. These feelings must be alleviated if the individual is to function successfully.[18]

It is in this context, says Fromm, that Lutheranism and Calvinism must be understood. They gave expression, not only to the new feeling of freedom, but to the accompanying feeling of anxiety and powerlessness. "The compulsive quest for certainty, as we find with Luther . . . is rooted in the need to conquer the unbearable doubt." His solution is to eliminate the isolated, individual self "by becoming an instrument in the hands of an overwhelmingly strong power outside the individual. For Luther this power was God and in unqualified submission he sought certainty."

Calvin's theology exhibits a great deal of this same spirit. He expresses vigorous opposition to the authority of the church and the blind acceptance of its doctrines; yet his religion is rooted in the powerlessness of man. The doctrine of predestination expresses the feeling of powerlessness and insignificance of the individual, and at the same time serves to quiet the doubts, for it is not difficult to believe that one is among the chosen—hence cannot do anything to endanger his own salvation. Yet "the doubt remained in the background and had to be silenced again and again by an ever-growing fanatic belief that the religious community to which one belonged represented that part of mankind which had been chosen by God." [19]

Fromm's analysis cannot be thought of as conclusive, for in *post factum* explanations, no matter how brilliant, one can never be certain that important variables have not been overlooked. Even if it is looked upon only as insightful speculation, however, it is a sharp formulation of a hypothesis that may be of great value when applied to contemporary religious developments. The analysis of the personality factors in communism and anticommunism might well profit by use of these insights.

More recent social psychological research on religious questions often applies concepts developed in studies of nonreligious activity. The tendency is to deal with limited populations and to gather new observations, by interview and questionnaire, to test specific propositions. Are there differences, Lenski asks, among Protestants, Catholics, and Jews in the Detroit area in their achievement motivation and in their acceptance of the deferred gratification pattern, when education and class have been controlled? (We shall not discuss his findings here, except to note that he found significant differences.) Similar questions are raised by McClelland, who has been the key person in the study of achievement motivation, and by several others. Their empirical work is giving strength to the social psychological dimension of religious research.[20]

To conclude this list of research areas, I will mention only briefly several other topics of importance and indicate some of the questions related to them. Sociologists are busily engaged in the study of groups of all kinds. Many of the concepts derived from small group research, reference group theory, and the analysis of large-scale organizations have relevance for the sociology of religion. How does a congregational as contrasted with a hierarchical structure affect a religious organization? What does it mean "to belong" to a church—is it the sort of segmental contact that one makes with many associations or is it a close personal attachment? How does this vary among the adherents of various religions, among classes, among those with different personal needs?

We are beginning to see the study of religious leaders in ways that go beyond the typological procedures of Weber and Wach.[21] Who become religious professionals? What various roles do they occupy in different societies, classes, and religious systems? What role conflicts do they face? How are variations in training, income, and identification with others manifest in their activity? To what degree do they prevent or initiate changes in religious belief and practice as a result of the interactions within the colleague group? The elaboration of a religious system has some immanent quality. This can be studied most effectively perhaps by analysis of the groups, the agencies of communication, the cultural forces that operate within the circle of religious leaders.

Most of the research areas I have mentioned so far apply to a wide range of types of societies. Some problems in the sociology of religion are concerned more specifically with modern urban societies, and some with American society only. What are the religious effects of spatial and social mobility? Certainly the "other-directed" man or the "organization man" leads a different life, religiously, from his predecessors. Is the church one of the new roots of the residents of suburbia, as Whyte suggests? Does it reduce or only reflect anomie? We have long discussed the differences between the "religions of the disinherited" and the "theodicy of good fortune" of those on top. Perhaps now we need an analysis of the religious lives of those who are moving up. From what do they want to be saved? What roads to salvation have meaning for them? If it is true that the major religious groups have strong communal solidarity, is this a temporary or a long-run phenomenon? Among whom is it especially apparent, among whom is it weak? Is this part of an effort to find for one's self "a brand name," as Herberg puts it? How is it related to the question of national unity, to nationalism, and the transfer of religious feeling to "the American way of life"? In broader terms, what conditions lead to conversion to a dominant religion or a convergence of religious traditions, what conditions lead to vigorous assertion of distinctive religious traditions?

Religion is inevitably affected by the types of communication available in a society. In the United States today, religious groups make extensive use of all the mass media. How do the media affect the types of materials used, the audiences, belief and action? [22] Has the balance of religious influence been affected by the fact that some groups employ the mass media extensively, others scarcely at all? What transformations occur in a religion that is presented in written form, orally to small groups, to large audiences through TV?

III. Conclusion

The research areas that I have mentioned do not constitute a systematic research program, because the list of problems could be greatly extended, because many of the questions raised are tied inextricably to others not listed, and above all because the need within each area is for the formulation of specific hypotheses capable of definitive testing. The range of problems that I have sketched may, however, suggest the potentialities and the significance of sociological studies of religion. It may also indicate the steps necessary for improvement in our understanding of religious phenomena: more explicit awareness of the problems of methodology, integration of the work of those who have been primarily concerned with theoretical formulations and those largely interested in gathering data, a fuller use of research and concepts from other areas—personality theory, the sociology of knowledge, theories of culture and cultural change, studies of bureaucracy, and the sociology of conflict, for example.

If one were to assess the resources available to the sociology of religion today, they might be listed somewhat as follows:

1. Some ambitious and often useful large-scale theoretical propositions. These have perhaps been too ambitious, based on too few data. We might be better served by "theories of the middle range."

2. A great deal of church and other religious history, often containing interpretative insights which, if rephrased, could serve as hypotheses. We have noted above the difficulties involved in building an empirical science on historical materials.

3. A rather large accumulation of facts in addition to church history—data on church membership, groups from which membership is drawn, denominational differences, recent social movements. Since much of this was gathered without reference to specific theoretical problems, it is often less useful than it might be.

4. Extensive anthropological material, often accompanied by theoretical propositions and interpretations. These have seldom been posed in testable hypotheses but are rich in guiding insights.

5. A few specifically sociological concepts and typolo-

gies that have proved useful in interpreting limited ranges of data.

6. An emerging general theory of personality, society, and culture that, when applied to the sociology of religion, sharpens its hypotheses and assists in organizing the data.

7. And, finally, one must add, we have some studies that make rather full use of the above—and other—resources to indicate the possibility, and indeed the great importance, of a thoroughly adequate sociology of religion.

FOOTNOTES

1. Merton, Robert K. *Social Theory and Social Structure*. The Free Press, 1949, p. 199.
2. *Ibid.*, p. 200.
3. *Ibid.*, p. 203.
4. Nadel, S. F. "Two Nuba Religions: An Essay in Comparison," *American Anthropologist*, vol. 57, no. 4 (1955), pp. 661-679; Anthony F. C. Wallace, "Revitalization Movements," *American Anthropologist*, vol. 58, no. 2 (1956), pp. 264-281; and the test of Weber's thesis in Japan by Robert N. Bellah, *Tokugawa Religion*, The Free Press, 1957.
5. See Peter and Alice Rossi, "Parochial School Education in America," *Daedalus*, Spring, 1961, pp. 300-328; Joseph Fichter, *Parochial School*, University of Notre Dame Press, 1958; Merton, *op. cit.*, Part IV.
6. See Gerhard Lenski, *The Religious Factor*, Doubleday and Co., 1961; L. H. Fuchs, *The Political Behavior of American Jews*, The Free Press, 1956; Luke Ebersole, "Religion and Politics," *Annals of the American Academy*, Nov., 1960, vol. 332, pp. 101-111.
7. See John J. Kane, *Catholic-Protestant Conflicts in America*, Regnery, 1955; Kenneth Underwood, *Protestant and Catholic*, The Beacon Press, 1957; and Don J. Hager, Charles Y. Glock, and Isidor Chein, eds., "Religious Conflict in the United States," *The Journal of Social Issues*, vol. XII, no. 3 (1956).
8. Pope, Liston. *Millhands and Preachers*. Yale University Press, 1942, pp. 86-88.
9. May, Henry F. *Protestant Churches and Industrial America*. Harper & Brothers, 1949, p. 93.

10. Quoted in David K. Petegorsky, *Left-Wing Democracy in the English Civil War*, Victor Gollancz, 1940, p. 179.

11. Quoted in G. P. Gooch, *English Democratic Ideas in the Seventeenth Century*, 2nd ed., University Press, 1927, p. 187.

12. See, e.g., Pope's study, *op. cit.*

13. Holt, John B. "Holiness Religion: Cultural Shock and Social Reorganization," *American Sociological Review*, Oct., 1940, vol. 5, p. 740.

14. Weber, Max. *The Protestant Ethic and the Spirit of Capitalism*. George Allen & Unwin, 1930, p. 172.

15. Durkheim, Emile. *The Elementary Forms of the Religious Life*. George Allen & Unwin, 1915, p. 327.

16. We are beginning to get valuable studies of the relationship of morality to religion. See, for example, Russell Middleton and Snell Putney, "Religion, Normative Standards, and Behavior," *Sociometry*, vol. 25, June, 1962, pp. 141-152; Robert W. Freidrichs, "Alter *Versus* Ego: An Exploratory Assessment of Altruism," *American Sociological Review*, Aug., 1960, vol. 25, pp. 496-508; Rose Golden, *et al.*, *What College Students Think*, Van Nostrand Co., 1960.

17. *Personality: A Biosocial Approach to Origins and Structure*. Harper & Brothers, 1947, p. 891.

18. Fromm, Erich. *Escape from Freedom*. New York: Rinehart & Co., 1941, pp. 62-63.

19. *Ibid.*, pp. 88-89.

20. See Lenski, *op. cit.*; David C. McClelland, *The Achieving Society*, Van Nostrand Co., 1961; Bernard Rosen, "Race, Ethnicity, and the Achievement Syndrome," *American Sociological Review*, Feb., 1959, vol. 24, pp. 47-60; Joseph Veroff, Sheila Field, and Gerald Gurin, "Achievement Motivation and Religious Background," *American Sociological Review*, April, 1962, vol. 27, pp. 205-217; Albert J. Mayer and Harry Sharp, "Religious Preference and Worldly Success," *American Sociological Review*, April, 1962, vol. 27, pp. 218-227.

21. See, for example, Samuel Blizzard, "The Roles of the Rural Parish Minister, the Protestant Seminaries, and the Science of Social Behavior," *Religious Education*, Nov.-Dec., 1955, pp. 1-10; Waldo W. Burchard, "Role Conflicts of Military Chaplains," *American Sociological Review*, Oct., 1954, pp. 528-535; Joseph Fichter, "The Religious Professional," *Review of Religious Research*, Winter, 1960, pp. 89-101 and Spring, 1960, pp. 150-170; H. Richard Niebuhr, Daniel D. Williams, and James M. Gustafson, *The Advancement of*

Theological Education, Harper & Brothers, 1957; James O. Smith and Gideon Sjoberg, "Origins and Career Patterns of Leading Protestant Clergymen," *Social Forces*, May, 1961, vol. 39, pp. 290-296.

22. See Everett C. Parker, David W. Barry, and Dallas W. Smythe, *The Television-Radio Audience and Religion*, Harper & Brothers, 1955.

7

The Function and Control of Power in the Church

ONE OF the assumptions of this book is that the analysis of religious groups can be strengthened by making use of concepts and research procedures developed with reference to nonreligious groups. Sociology, economics, and political science share interest in the study of the administrative procedures, the formal organizations, the bureaucracies so characteristic of modern societies. A key question in the study of large-scale organizations concerns the location of power within them. Who makes the basic decisions? Toward what goals is the power directed? What conditions maximize the possibility that the goals of the organization will be achieved? Is it inevitable that a small group will gain control, even of presumably democratic organizations, as the result of the operation of some "iron law of oligarchy," or a "Parkinson's law"?

In this chapter we shall attempt to illustrate the way in which general social scientific concepts apply to a religious organization. If our assumption is correct, such questions as those we have noted above should be as relevant to the study of large-scale religious organizations as to the study of industrial or governmental bureaucracies. In each case, study of the location and use of power is fundamental to the understanding of the organization.

Power is found in all human relations and is *per se* neither good nor evil. It can be thought of as a motor the effect of which is known only when its connection with a steering mechanism is known. The word "power" often carries mild or even strong negative connotations, usually by association with highly coercive, violent, or concentrated forms of power. We shall use it as a neutral term.

We shall need to be alert to the ways in which the question of power is different in an organization whose goals are unambiguous (there is only the problem of the technical efficiency of means) from what it is in an organization whose goals themselves are constantly under debate. The World Council of Churches eschews unity of worship; yet few of its participants would be content with a definition of its aim as a search for moral unity—agreement on goals and methods concerned with human interaction. Many a conference and paper has sought to answer the question: "What is the nature of the unity we seek?" Clearly the function and control of power in such an organization are different from what they are in an organization with relatively more sharply defined goals (for example, the National Association for the Advancement of Colored People). One should not forget, of course, that latent, undefined goals may complicate the situation in groups that seem to be entirely unified in aim.

The problem of ambiguity of goals can be put in another way: Religious organizations are used, both intentionally and unintentionally, in the pursuit of goals other than religious ones. This is true both for the laymen who support and the professionals who lead. Ecumenicalism is undoubtedly affected by the nonreligious functions that churches serve for individuals and groups. The wide variation in the forms of religious organization and practice that appeal to different individuals and groups indicates— among other things—the differences in secular needs and tendencies. Ernst Troeltsch, Richard Niebuhr, and many others have shown the ways in which religious unity and disunity are affected by secular unity and disunity. There is a wealth of research to indicate that differences in class and race, in nationality, in personality, in position in the economic and political system, and many other aspects of secular society influence the type of religious group one will support. No clear line can be drawn between a religious and a nonreligious use of a religious organization; but it is certain that failure to recognize the extent to which men invest many different kinds of hopes in their religious groups will lead to inadequate understanding of our topic.

I. From Prophet to Priest

In the analysis of power, it is well to note that different questions arise at different stages in the life of an organization. There is likely to be a shift in the nature of leadership, growth in the complexity of the structure of the organization, and changes in the pattern of interaction with other groups. Each of these affects the power situation.

In its early years, an organization may be led by persons who are opposed to some aspects of the prevailing structure. A major leader of a new movement "preaches, creates, or demands *new* obligations," as Weber put it. But whether or not there are major or minor prophets, with an abundance of charisma, there will be persons moved by an exciting vision of something better, as they see it. Their task is not to operate an organization, but to build one. To the degree that they succeed, however, they change the nature of the leadership likely to be found and needed in the organization. A staff is assembled to keep records, to carry on the functions that have been set in motion, and to keep the organization vigorous.

The job conceptions of this "second generation" of leaders tend to be different from those of the first generation. They feel themselves identified not so much with the problem or task for which the group was first formed, but with the organization itself. They are also more likely to be concerned with orderly careers for themselves, with the preservation of their power (which usually requires the maintenance of the structure of the organization), with the maintenance of appropriate status positions.

We are referring here to what is usually called "goal displacement," the deflection of effort from the original purpose. Philip Selznick calls this "the organizational paradox" and notes how often the aims of a group are frustrated by its appearance. The dedication and enthusiasm of the founders do not hold up, there is a "routinization of charisma," in Weber's terms, as attention is shifted from the original goals to the organization that has been set up presumably to achieve those goals. It is one thing, for example, to be dedicated to ecumenical work, it is another thing to be dedicated to the World Council of Churches—and in the shift, the original purpose may get absorbed into many diverse interests related to the organization, and may be partly obscured, changed, even contradicted by these diverse interests.

Sills well describes the problem of goal preservation in these words:

In order to accomplish their goals, organizations establish a set of procedures, or means. In the course of following these procedures, however, the subordinates or members to whom authority and functions have been delegated often come to regard them as ends in themselves, rather than as means toward the achievement of organization goals. As a result of this process, the actual activities of the organization become centered around the proper functioning of organization procedures, rather than upon the achievement of the initial goals.[1]

There is no reason to suppose that religious organizations are not affected by this process of a shift from "charismatic" to "bureaucratic" leadership—to put the matter in excessively sharp terms. In a relatively young organization

like the World Council, there is likely to be far more
concern with problems of defining goals than there is with
deflection from goals. But this may not long be true. Religious groups often resist the implication that their staffs
are concerned with orderly career patterns, with status,
with power.[2] Failure to recognize these interests compli-
cates the problem of deflection rather than eliminating it.
Some of the difficulties encountered in getting cooperation
among established religious groups, however they may be
explained by reference to differences in principle, often indicate an attachment to procedure.

The question of shift in type of leadership as an organization grows in size and complexity is part of a series of
questions that the student of power must ask concerning
leadership. From what source are the leaders of an organization drawn, and with what results? With reference to
churches there would be various answers, of course. In
the United States, the Protestant clergy is drawn in larger
than proportionate numbers from small towns in the Middle West. Little is known about the consequences of this
fact, although there are some hypotheses; but this and
similar facts deserve careful study. After something is
known of the sources of leaders, it is well to inquire about
the criteria used and the processes of selection for movement up various church ladders. Do individuals move up
who are mainly talented at denominational work, or is
there selection of persons inclined toward ecumenicalism?
Put in another way, which churches will most vigorously
back their men in the work of interdenominational groups?
This should be seen as one case of a general question:
What social conditions select leaders who are narrow or
broad in their concerns? A "politically ecumenical leader"
(if I may use this awkward phrase) at the head of Egypt
today is difficult to imagine. The poverty, the powerlessness, the lack of information of the great majority of Egyp-
tians inevitably narrow the goals of their leaders and impose severe limits on the kinds of policies they can pursue

and still remain in power. It would be highly desirable to explore the ways in which the constituencies of religious leaders affect the kinds of goals they may pursue.

II. Power in Relation to Outside Influences

The location of power varies among different types of social structure. Loosely federated organizations (doubtless the World Council would be placed in this classification) have advantages and disadvantages in the accomplishment of their goals when compared with unified organizations. Churches that are structurally separate from the state gain some kinds of influence and lose other kinds. Agencies (religious or otherwise) that succeed in expanding their influence may find they have paid a price in deflection from their goals. Let us examine some of the issues involved in these statements.

David Truman argues (see *The Government Process*, 1951) that federated organizations are less able to influence the course of government—are less powerful—than unified or corporate type organizations. The former cannot so easily present a united front. This is especially true when the units in the federation preceded it historically. Such a situation is true of contemporary ecumenical organizations which, by the fact of their federated quality, speak with less direct influence. On the other hand, unified organizations often restrict policy discussion, allow less room for new ideas and growth of policy, work less easily with other organizations with whom they might share some interest. These points may be illustrated by noting that the United Nations, a federated body, is unable to take various kinds of action today, because of the "sovereignty" of its constituent parts. Yet most persons would agree that it could be unified only by suppressing some of the diverse elements now within it, thus defeating many of its major purposes.

Whatever their advantages and weaknesses, federated organizations frequently move toward more consolidated types. It is perhaps too much to say that federated organizations are inherently unstable and short-lived. It is certainly true, however, that wherever they seek influence beyond their own internal affairs, they exhibit a tendency toward a unified or corporate structure. Unless those empowered to make decisions can act definitively, when vital questions arise, they may lose opportunities to answer those questions in ways satisfactory to the organization. Even a democracy, which in ideology is a federation (in the American case a federation of "sovereign" states and in every case of "sovereign" individuals who yield their power only temporarily and on a limited basis to the decision makers), tends to move toward a corporate structure when relations with other states become continuous and vital. To put the matter in overly simple terms: under many circumstances, a federated, loosely knit organization maintains greater flexibility, allows more of its constituent elements to express themselves—but is often unable to arrive at a policy, or if it achieves a policy, is relatively unable to act upon it. A unified organization, on the other hand, can achieve and act upon policy—but at the cost of power concentration.

There are two aspects to this power dilemma. One deals with the way in which an organization is related to other groups; the other is concerned with the distribution of power within the organization. Let us examine each of these briefly in terms of general principles, and then make some application to churches.

As an organization seeks to broaden its influence, it usually must win the support of other agencies and persons who are only partly in agreement with its aims. There are times when a group must try to neutralize the influence of some power that is strongly opposed to its program. For example, the Tennessee Valley Authority, dedicated to the unified planning of a region, found in the area other agencies with which it had to deal. Farmer organizations, state governments, private business interests, et cetera, had their own ideas and interests on many of the same subjects with which the Tennessee Valley Authority was concerned. The TVA could not simply disregard them and expect to be effective, for these groups possessed economic and political power. Instead, the staff of the TVA sought to involve as many as possible of the existing groups into the planning and execution of its own program—to co-opt them, to win their support. It would take us too far from our central interest to explore the result of this process of co-optation. We shall have to be content with the statement that most social scientists would probably agree that within four or five years after its founding, the original plan of the TVA had been severely modified by the compromises insisted upon by the various co-opted groups. One aspect of the original plan was not modified—production of electrical power by a public agency; and TVA had won some other victories. But in most respects, TVA had settled into the framework of the existing power structure insofar as it involved farm tenancy, the public ownership of land (beyond that necessary for the dams), Negro-white relations, and other questions.[3]

Applications of the principle of co-optation abound in the history of religious organizations. One thinks immediately of Troeltsch's well known remark concerning the church: "It dominates the world and is therefore dominated by the world." One thinks of the National Conference of Christians and Jews in the United States, an agency that sometimes shows so much interest in winning the support of Southern businessmen for the symbols of Brotherhood Week that it says little, in that area, about desegregation; or is so eager to get the cooperation of New York industrialists that it refrains from asking them why some of them employ no Jews. (This remark should not be read as a general evaluation of the program of the NCCJ.)

If failure to win the support of powerful secular organizations means relative powerlessness and if the effort to win their support runs the danger of co-optation, religious organizations face a serious dilemma. This dilemma is found most sharply, perhaps, in the relationships between churches and states. Those who believe that clear separation of church and state increases the power of the church emphasize the freedom from political domination, the freedom to criticize the political process and the secular power structure. There is the danger, however, that such freedoms are closely connected with powerlessness. On the other hand, close institutional connection between church and state scarcely avoids the dilemma, because the union raises the likelihood that the church will be used to lend sanctity to a secular power structure. The problem is to find a way to be simultaneously in politics (thus to influence it) and beyond politics (thus free to challenge it).

Such a goal requires an exploration of the conditions under which religious power can achieve maximum autonomy. Without being able to develop the reasoning that lies behind the remark, let me state that the dilemma of a religious organization is least sharp in a society where the average man has some measure of economic security, has political instruments for expressing his judgments, and has unhampered sources of information on which to base his decisions—in short, in a society where secular power is widely diffused. If this is true, religious organizations can maximize their power best by helping to create the kind of society where they are not caught in an unhappy choice between irrelevance and extensive compromise.

If these remarks seem, at the moment, to be far removed from the problems of the World Council of Churches, they may nevertheless bear on problems of the future. As the World Council moves down the road from unity at the conference level, to more and more firm pronouncements on Christian positions with respect to crucial issues, to efforts to procure action on these issues, the problem of power will become more difficult. To get the action desired will require the cooperation of other agencies and persons with a wide range of values. To win the support of nations, of universities, of labor unions will be to run the risk of having the Council's goals sharply redefined. To fail to try to win their support will be to give up the task of accomplishing certain goals.

III. Power Distribution Within an Organization

The second aspect of the power dilemma concerns the distribution of power within an organization. As the structure of a group becomes more complex, there is a tendency, under many conditions, for the majority to lose influence to a small core of individuals who manage the organization. For some purposes, this development may be of little importance; there may be little need for mass participation; expert knowledge and action are all that is required. "Salvation" from malaria can be achieved by the efforts of a small number of research scientists, doctors, drug manufacturers, and pilots. This is not true of religious organizations: to accomplish their goals ordinarily requires the active cooperation of the whole range of the membership. We must ask, therefore, what conditions keep the largest number of individuals personally involved in the pursuit of the goals of an organization; what conditions lead to membership apathy?

There is an extensive literature on this subject, ranging from the overly hasty generalization of Pareto, Mosca, Michels, and others concerning an "iron law of oligarchy" (the phrase comes from Michels and is used with reference to political parties) to detailed studies of specific groups. Weber's work on bureaucracy is carefully grounded in empirical study, but it also tends to describe a process that occurs under some conditions as if it were an "iron law." More recently, detailed examination of power location within specific organizations by Gouldner, by Lipset, Trow and Coleman, by Sills, and others is beginning to build more adequate conceptions.[4]

Lipset, Trow, and Coleman for example, ask the classic question: Under what conditions is democracy possible? Their primary concern is with labor unions, but they offer evidence that has broader applicability. A group with a large middle class with approximately equal income can resist oligarchic tendencies, as Aristotle taught us. It is perhaps also true that diffused power is more characteristic of small groups. But these two principles alone are not adequate, for both large and heterogeneous groups may be democratic. The principle of pluralism is also important: democracy is possible where organized subgroups (none with majority power) compete in a context of mutual tolerance and with some sense of common identity with the whole group.

There is widespread agreement on the proposition that as organizations grow in size, in the need for functionally specialized roles, in membership heterogeneity, there is increased likelihood that power will be concentrated in fewer hands (see Sills, 1957). There is no reason to suppose that religious organizations are free from these influences. Policy making is likely to be "delegated upward"— to national or international conventions, composed of those persons most concerned with the problem in hand. But many kinds of action are of necessity "delegated downward," to local churches and individuals. Difficult as it is to get agreement on broad principles on the national and international level, it often proves even more difficult to get action on the local level. The individuals who must carry out the action are often less concerned. But even where they are deeply interested in the issue, they find themselves surrounded by a different set of forces from those that influenced the policy makers. The persons with whom they work are often more closely identified with their job, their family, their class and region, their nation, than they are with their church—and these various groups may well make conflicting demands. It is a common thing in the United States to read of the support given by a national or even a Southern regional church conference to the Supreme Court ruling on school desegregation. It is a very uncommon thing to hear of a local church taking such a stand in the area where the issue is controversial. The kinds of forces acting upon local church leaders are clearly different in some ways from those acting upon leaders of regional, national, and international groups. In technical terms, their "reference groups" are different.[5]

It would seem that this question of "the flow of power" —from the individual and local group upward to the international organization, and from that body downward to the local situation again—must be of great importance to the World Council. The identification of the conditions that promote control of an organization by an active minority and those that keep a large proportion of the membership involved require continuing study. The active minority may win many "paper victories," because it overlooks the apathy or opposition of the majority. One may come away from a conference feeling exhilarated by the agreements reached (often painfully), only to discover that one has been misled by what Robert Merton has called "the fallacy of group soliloquy"—the feeling of unanimity reached by a small minority unmindful of their relative isolation.

It is not necessarily true, of course, that "mass apathy" or indifference represents failure. One should perhaps draw a distinction between an apathy of contentment and an apathy of powerlessness. (Berelson, Lazarsfeld, and McPhee develop the thesis that the presence of a large block of nonvoters in the United States, as compared with

France for example, has positive functions for the maintenance of a stable democratic government.) [6] It would be an unusual case, however, in a religious organization, in which personal involvement of the largest possible number would not be thought to be desirable.

Thus the study of power in the church can be informed by the application of the concepts of social science. The church cannot escape the dilemmas of power.[7] In its efforts to reduce their sharpness, it may be more successful by approaching its problems indirectly, than by direct confrontation of other powers. That is, the efforts of religious organizations might best be directed toward the creation of conditions within which decisions in harmony with their goals will most readily be made by individuals and groups acting in their various social roles.

FOOTNOTES

1. Sills, David L. *The Volunteers*. The Free Press, 1957, p. 62.
2. For an excellent study of the way contemporary theory of bureaucracy can be applied to a church organization (in this instance the American Baptist Convention) see Paul M. Harrison, *Authority and Power in the Free Church Tradition*, Princeton University Press, 1959.
3. See especially Philip Selznick, *TVA and the Grass Roots*, University of California Press, 1949.
4. See Alvin W. Gouldner, *Patterns of Industrial Bureaucracy*, The Free Press, 1954; S. M. Lipset, Martin Trow, and James Coleman, *Union Democracy*, The Free Press, 1956; Sills, *op. cit.*
5. Campbell, E. Q. and T. F. Pettigrew. "Racial and Moral Crisis: The Role of Little Rock Ministers," *American Journal of Sociology*, March, 1959, vol. LXIV, pp. 509-516.
6. Berelson, B. R., P. F. Lazarsfeld, and W. N. McPhee. *Voting*. University of Chicago Press, 1954.
7. See Thomas F. O'Dea, "Five Dilemmas in the Institutionalization of Religion," and the comment that follows by J. Milton Yinger, *Journal for the Scientific Study of Religion*, Oct., 1961, vol. 1, pp. 30-41.

Conclusion

JOHN DEWEY once remarked that every thinker puts some portion of an apparently stable world in peril. The history of the relationship between science and religion supports this statement: first physics and astronomy, then biology, and now sociology and psychology have brought into question some of the assumptions of a stable religious world view. But this fact requires careful interpretation. The clash has led some persons to say: therefore the findings of science must be denied, or attacked, or declared irrelevant. It has led others to affirm: the findings of science have demonstrated the falsity of religious beliefs. What neither of these two groups has explained, however, is the fact that after centuries of presumed serious conflict, both science and religion continue to prosper. This is true, I believe, because these two aspects of man's life do not and cannot clash in any fundamental way; they represent different areas of human endeavor. Science is an effort to understand the world; religion is an effort to respond to life, to act in such a way as to give meaning to the human condition. It is clear that each affects the other; each sets conditions within which the other is developed. Religion in a scientific era will speak in a different idiom, it will develop new systems of "overbeliefs" by means of which men struggle with the basic problems of life. But it is no more true to say that science destroys religion than it is to say that science destroys art. When new media of communication, new materials, new instruments are invented, science sets new conditions within which artistic life is carried on; it modifies the forms of expression; but it does not destroy the expressive and creative process.

This analogy may suggest two things. Many persons will say, of the new forms of art or religion, "do you call *that* art or religion?" The various answers would indicate the second thing. Not all religion, or art, is good, by the standards of a given person or group. The religious forms that are developing in the context of science may not be meaningful and creative ones; too much that was rich may be lost or too much that has lost its significance may be retained. But of this we can be certain: by the growth of knowledge, religion will be changed, yet it will not be destroyed. Social science will surely modify contemporary religious expressions in many ways, but it will no more destroy religion or satisfy the needs from which religion springs than has astronomy.

Just how the growth of social science will modify religion it is difficult to guess. I would speculate that if the scientific view of the world were to become widespread (in my judgment, no truly "scientific society" has yet developed—so few of us are interested in or able to make more than a few of our judgments on the basis of the evidence), these criteria would become significant to men in arriving at their religious judgments:

Does the religion in question get involved in the full range of problems related to the human condition? Specialized attention to health, loneliness, powerlessness, or even man's finiteness is not likely to be the basis of a religion that is widely accepted and long-lived.

Is the religion capable of being restated when life's

conditions change? This may be to ask the same question, for it also refers to questions of scope and flexibility. Some religious expressions are narrowly local and temporal, and unable to establish their relevance to new conditions.

Does the religion fit harmoniously with the best of man's contemporary thinking and expression in intellectual, artistic, and moral endeavors, as the best is defined by the group in question? Is it, in other words, capable of growth and development?

There is no certainty that a religion which meets such criteria will become dominant. I am only speculating that in a society where science had become a vital part of the world view of most people, either religious expressions in harmony with that fact would develop, or religious substitutes only marginally able to help us deal with the human condition would prevail.

Let me end on a problem and a question. Even as many efforts are being made, against strong obstacles, for "ecumenicalism" within Christendom, the world becomes so thoroughly interactive that the need is clearly for a world ecumenicalism. (Forgive the redundant adjective. But do we not need to underline how partial are the current efforts toward ecumenicalism?) While Lutheran and Anglican and Presbyterian wonder under what circumstances and on what issues they may work together, and while Pope John calls for a conclave for all Christian churches, an even larger question appears: Under what circumstances and on what issues can Christian churches work together with other religious groups? What are the implications— for religion and for man—of the fact that many faiths are now in constant confrontation, and that each, however gracious and tolerant it may be toward others, tends to insist upon its unique hold upon the truth? Is religious modesty possible, or is this simply a courteous way of pointing to "indifferentism"? Is it possible to hold tentative convictions? And what are the consequences of various possible answers to these questions? In dealing with the individual and group powers of the world, religion finds itself working in a constantly more complicated situation. To define the tasks and accept the forms of expression that may have had meaning a century or even a decade ago may be to court utter failure in a world in which the aim of brotherhood has suddenly been transformed from an exciting vision to an absolute necessity.